Asinof, Eliot, 1919-
    People vs. Blutcher; black and white law
in Bedford-Stuyvesant.   New York, Viking
Press [1970]
    xiii, 239 p.   22cm.

    1. Blutcher, Laurence, 1937-
2. Negroes--   Brooklyn.   I. Title.

PEOPLE VS. BLUTCHER

People vs.

BLACK MEN AND WHITE LAW

Eliot

NEW YOR

Blutcher

IN BEDFORD–STUYVESANT

Asinof

THE VIKING PRESS

First published in 1970 by The Viking Press, Inc.
625 Madison Avenue, New York, N.Y. 10022

Published simultaneously in Canada by
The Macmillan Company of Canada Limited

SBN 670-54792-1

Library of Congress catalog card number: 74-109218

Printed in U.S.A. by Vail-Ballou Press, Inc.

For Larry

"Cops are like twenty-dollar whores. Sometimes you think you need 'em, but they ain't never worth it."

—Overheard in a Bedford-Stuyvesant barber shop

"We didn't land on Plymouth Rock; Plymouth Rock landed on us."

—Malcolm X

FOREWORD

In the black ghettoes of America, law and order is a farce. The relationship of police and civilians is akin to an undeclared war wherein the "occupied" citizens have never known it any other way. It is a war that touches them all, some brutally, as all wars do, leaving scars that cut deeply into the mores of their lives; and the resulting chaos appears to have become as absolute and irrevocable as death and taxes.

The problem begins with race and dates back to slavery. "If you're white you're right, if you're black go back." This is our heritage and the ghetto is its outgrowth. To the blacks, the basic meaning of race is poverty. Poverty is the key that locks the black man in, and the culture of the ghetto is the struggle to surmount it. It is a relentless struggle that few can win, made all the more gruesome by the colossal titillation of television, exacerbating the black man's frustrations with its enticements of glamorous possessions and a life of affluence. In the end, it leads to confusion and crime and violence, and, above all, keeps him from becoming a man.

The quest for manhood is not a simple thing in any community, but in such areas as Bedford-Stuyvesant in Brooklyn it is as difficult as an escape from prison. At thirty, a black man is defeated and a black woman is an unloved mother. The ghetto is always dominated by youth; far more than the national average, the majority in the black communities of America is under thirty. As a result, the action is what happens on the streets, and when a youth graduates from them, he has his diploma into adulthood but he is not necessarily a man. His entire experience is likely to be circumscribed by a series of predictably dehumanizing incidents: gang rumbles, quickie sex in tenement hallways, petty thievery, menial jobs at meager pay, and a number of abusive confrontations with the law. Indeed, his relationship with the police is the most predictable of all. It is also likely to be the most brutal.

The story of one Laurence Blutcher at the age of thirty reflects the essence of this experience. At its core is such a confrontation with police, and, brutal though it was, it is no accident that no attention was paid—another dog-bites-man story, as it were—by the major newspapers of New York City. It was hardly strange, then, that my own inquiries attracted incredulous responses from his family and friends: "Why do you want to write about this?" I was asked. "It happens every day around here."

This, of course, became the strength of the story. The frequency with which the Larry Blutchers of America suffer these experiences supplies its special meaning and demands our attention. The literature of our times is already rich with the drama of violent black rebellion and the extraordinary histories of such contentious heroes as Malcolm X, Eldridge Cleaver, Dick Gregory, Claude Brown—all men with an uncommon capacity to climb above the squalor of their backgrounds. To read them is unique and inspirational, but it tends to distort the common experience, since they are so superior to it. Similarly, one cannot create a true image of white American society from the biographies of Richard Nixon, Bob Hope, Thomas Watson, or Joe

Willie Namath. If it is true that any citizen can become President of the United States—or the richest entertainer in Hollywood—the odds are not likely to influence many to give their lives to it. It takes a Larry Blutcher to render the common truth. What he has to say details not only the way it is but the way it is changing. He is the foot soldier in the war, and his story is told from the vantage point of all the mud, sweat, and drudgery that are the fate of many.

I met him shortly after the violent incident that is the focal point of this book, then spent the eighteen months that led to its resolution digging into his history. It was a difficult period for him, as the reader will learn, a period of startling changes in his orientation, a growth toward a fresh understanding of what it is to be a man in the face of what "the system" does to choke him. If the reader can benefit but a fraction of what I experienced in pursuing this account, my efforts will have been amply justified.

We are living at a time when Americans think of the ghetto with such shame and opprobrium, we tend to forget there are real, live people trapped in them, fighting for whatever dignity they can hope to achieve. This is the story of one such man.

PEOPLE VS. BLUTCHER

1

It was shortly after ten o'clock on the gray Sunday morning of December 3, 1967, when Laurence Blutcher walked down the creaking flight of stairs from his apartment onto the street and crossed the few yards to the adjacent store front. The L&S FOOD STORE sign arched neatly across the plate glass window, partially visible through the accordion iron gate that shielded it from potential thieves. L&S. Lafayette and Stuyvesant, named for the two old Brooklyn avenues that intersected in front. In this area of the Bedford-Stuyvesant community, the avenues betrayed the greatness of the men for whom they were named, an endless line of decrepit two-story houses and rubble-filled lots, of liquor stores and barber shops and groceries coated with the multi-layered filth of too many years of poverty.

Blutcher unlocked the iron gate and opened it just far enough to gain access to the door, musing of his mixed feelings about that gate. For one thing, it had cost him $300 to install, money he might have used to stock his shelves. For another, it was ugly.

Nonetheless, he accepted it as a necessity and he tried to think of it as a sturdy symbol of his permanence as a store owner.

"I went inside, then locked the door behind me. I wasn't going to open yet. Not after working so late, almost to midnight on Saturday, too late to tabulate before closing. I had to get the accounts straight before I began a new week. It wasn't easy because so much of my business was done on credit. Always on credit. I didn't have to do much adding, though, to know I didn't have a good week. Not even as good as the last one when I'd sold only $451 worth of merchandise."

The thought of a continued decline both bewildered and frightened him, and as he fumbled with his slips and receipts his hand brushed awkwardly against the counter, knocking his pencil to the floor. He climbed off his stool, and as he kneeled to recover it, he was startled by the sharp metallic rap of a finger ring against glass.

He looked up over the counter and saw the policeman through the window, the patrol car behind him. He thought he must have looked peculiar coming up from under the counter that way. Like a man who'd been hiding, perhaps, adding to his uneasiness because that wasn't his style. He hated the police. Especially on Sunday. But he would never hide from them.

He walked around the counter and unlocked the front door, knowing full well what was wanted of him. There was a blond patrolman standing there. Blutcher had seen him before but didn't know him. The dark-haired one was driving the car. That was Repaci, Blutcher knew. He knew Repaci. Yes, especially on Sunday. There was a Sabbath Law in New York State relating to stores' being open on Sunday, and the police were occasionally aware of it—albeit in various ways.

"In February, I was given a summons for the Sabbath Law violation. A cop walked in, wrote out a summons. 'Happy New Year,' he said to me and walked out. I had to go down to police court and pay a five-dollar fine, like the way you pay a parking ticket. But that was just the set-up. After they make you do that they come around and tell you 'It's the Sabbath, you can't be open—unless you know what you have to do.' Sure, I knew what I had to do. I had to pay them off. Two dollars each. Very cool, very businesslike. Everybody comes out ahead. Right?

"So now there was this blond policeman standing there, and Repaci was watching in the car. 'You planning to open today?' he asks me."

Blutcher stood there, holding the door partially open, enough to block the entrance. Was he planning to open today? The question galled him, the answer was that obvious. It was like asking a kid with spikes and a baseball glove if he was going to play ball. Every cop in Bedford-Stuyvesant knew that the neighborhood grocer did far more business on Sunday than on any other day and had to stay open to keep his business alive.

"I might," Blutcher replied, immediately annoyed at his own duplicity.

"Well, we'll be back if you do."

"Why don't you leave me alone?" That was better, there was a ring of defiance in his voice.

The policeman smiled. "We'll be back," he said and returned to the squad car, then disappeared around the corner of Stuyvesant Avenue.

Blutcher went back to work, but the confrontation stayed with him, rankling in him like a persistent toothache. He finished his bookkeeping, then straightened out a few items on his barren shelves. It was still early, too early to open, for there was very little action on the streets during winter Sunday mornings. Besides, he had not eaten breakfast. He decided he'd go to his older brother John's house where he could always get something to eat —and, in this instance, talk over what he ought to do.

John Blutcher was thirty-seven, almost seven years older than Larry, and a man with an intimate knowledge of the community. He was founder and leader of a self-help organization called Together We Stand with some 800 youngsters and their parents in a disciplined program designed to instill community pride. He knew how important it was to work with the police, but the concept of his brother being forced into a weekly shakedown did not seem justifiable.

" 'No, sir, you shouldn't pay them,' I advised him.

"My brother, he was very unhappy. He drank his coffee, ate some toast and jam, and kept shaking his head. He was very confused, like he couldn't make up his mind at all.

" 'Look, Bubba, you're closed on Mondays. You're not doing anything illegal. You shouldn't have to pay them.' [Bubba was the family nickname for Larry. John himself had to take the blame for that; he'd had a friend in school named Bubba and he started to call his baby brother by that name. The family simply picked it up.]

" 'Well, I ain't going to,' Larry said. "I ain't even taking in enough to pay off anything.' "

The nuances of a shakedown took a man on a strange and twisted morality: you paid off when you did something illegal —unless you were doing enough legitimate business to afford it.

"It seemed to relax him, saying that. He was glad to know I felt the same way. He called Vina [their older sister, whose real name is Earvina] and told her what he told me, and she told him the same as I did, not to pay off. When he hung up, he was smiling for the first time: Vina had told him that it was the cops who ought to be arrested! We laughed at that, both of us thinking that maybe we ought to send Vina down there to do the arresting. She is pretty near tough enough to pull it off."

The truth was, Larry was anything but relaxed. It was one of those periods when nothing seemed to be going right. Although he was 30 years old, he had solved none of the big problems in his life. He had hoped that the store would be the big steppingstone toward achieving a workable manhood, a base for his economic security. It was an independent, responsible, respectable occupation. Independent. That was the key thing. He could be his own boss, his own man. It was to be his achievement, accomplished by hard work and determination. He had hoped that the store would be a kind of home for himself and his woman, a momma-poppa enterprise, as he liked to put it, where they could share in the struggle to make it work together. But there was no woman. Even though he was married, there was no woman. His wife, Jacqueline, was gone. He hadn't seen her in six months. Six months since she had popped in on him, out of the blue, really, titillating him with her large soft eyes and her mellifluous voice and her beguiling style—only to pop right out again. Whatever interest she had in Larry, the store was not included. It was clear that she hated the store, the whole idea of it. She had left him alone with his troubles.

As he walked back down Lafayette Avenue from his brother's apartment, there were only troubles on his mind. Troubles compounded by loneliness.

"I used to wake up on Sunday and think, well, okay, this one was going to be the big day. The real big one. But it never happened. Not the way I wanted. After a while I could get a feeling about how I was going to do, like something blowing in the wind, and I just didn't have no high hopes no more. Hell, I didn't even have the stock on the shelves to do it.

"On this Sunday, I had the bad feeling. I passed a guy I knew, he was going into a place where they were having a crap game. It had been going on and off for weeks. I thought, wow, I used to get busted for shooting craps. I'd quit that whole kind of life years ago. No more gambling or hustles or stuff like that. Now the cops don't bust the crap games, but they come after me for trying to run a straight business. It was weird, all right. It could turn a man sour if you let it. I was glad of what John and Vina had told me, not to pay them off any more. I mean, it was what I felt like doing . . ."

When Blutcher returned to the store, it was a few minutes after one. He pushed aside the iron gate and opened up. Though it was beginning to rain, the weather was still mild and there were people moving about along the avenues. He sold a few candy bars to some kids, some bread and milk to a man, and then the familiar green and white patrol car pulled up to the curb.

" 'Well . . . ?' The blond policeman walked into the store. McCole was his name. Then Repaci came in, and the two of them stood there smiling, like they were embarrassed, maybe. 'I warned you about opening,' he said. I could feel the nerves building up inside me. It was decision time, all right.

" 'I'm not giving you anything,' I mumbled. I guess I didn't have the guts to say it right out.

" 'What?' McCole said, pretending he hadn't heard.

" 'Nothing. I'm not giving you nothing!' I said.

" 'Don't be a fool. I'll give you a summons.'

" 'Go ahead,' I said.

"Then Repaci put in his two cents. 'You gotta close this store or we're gonna give you a summons. Or you know what you have to do . . .'

" 'I'm not paying nobody off. I mean what I say,' I said, real loud, all of a sudden.

"Well, they walked around the store and kept telling me I had to close. I said I didn't have to. I wasn't violating the law. I wasn't selling no meats, no salami, no bacon—not until after four o'clock like the Sabbath Law says.

" 'Don't be such a wise cocksucker,' Repaci said.

" 'The best thing you can do is give me a summons and get out of my store.'

" 'All right,' McCole said. 'What's your name?'

" 'It's on the wall,' I pointed to the sign. LAURENCE BLUTCHER, PROP.

" 'Suppose you tell me,' he said, and then he called me 'a black motherfucker.'

"Well, that started a lot of yelling, and that began to fire me up. The noise was making the juices work inside me and the juices were making me mad. I could feel the strength from it. I wasn't gonna give them a damn thing.

8

" 'We're gonna take you in,' McCole shouted at me.

" 'Go ahead,' I shouted back.

" 'Get the sergeant,' he told Repaci.

" 'I don't care if you get the whole Precinct,' I said. 'I'm not paying off no more.' "

Suddenly, in the midst of this verbal skirmish, the front door opened. A tired middle-aged Negro walked in with his eleven-year-old son, a stout boy with a round cherubic face. The man immediately sensed the electricity in the store, though he had heard nothing, and moved quickly to the counter without so much as a glance at the policemen.

Bernard Trotta lived a few blocks away on Reid Avenue, and was on his way to visit a friend, Beverly Harris, directly across the street from the L&S Food Store.

"When I passed in front of Larry's store, I thought, heck, I was out of cigarettes. Sure, I saw the police car and that made me wonder some. But then, those guys are always around. It didn't mean nothing that they were around. But no sooner did I get inside when I saw there was trouble brewing. The two cops, they were standing there with that tough-cop look. There was nothing friendly about them. And Larry, I could see he didn't like it one bit.

" 'I know my rights,' he was saying. 'I ain't gonna give you a goddam thing.'

"The cops, they didn't say anything back. They just stood there, looking at me, waiting for me to get out. And Larry, he kept blasting away. I never seen him so mad before. 'You can call the whole damn Precinct if you want!' he said. So I took my cigarettes and hustled out, figuring there was business going on and it weren't none of mine. Ordinarily, I would've stopped to pass the time of day. But not with them there. Only thing, my son wanted a pickle. He saw those pickles on the counter and decided he wanted one. But I just kept ahold of him and pulled him right out of the store."

"When the Trottas left, the two went at me again. 'Let's get the sergeant,' McCole said again, and Repaci, he went out to the patrol car to make the call. I could see him through the window, and then he sat there, in the car, waiting for the sergeant. McCole, he just stood inside, waiting, too. I knew they were still trying to get money from me. He could have written the summons if he wanted to. He was standing no more than four feet from the sign with my name on it. He just stood there watching me, that's all. Cops, they're good at waiting. They can wait all day. Hell, they get paid for waiting.

"Pretty soon, maybe three or four minutes, the sergeant [Sergeant Joseph Gallante] drove up in a patrol car, and Repaci talked to him in the street. And then they came in. The sergeant, he walked up to me smiling like he was going to solve the whole thing.

" 'Are you gonna co-operate?' he said to me.

"I said I wanted to make a phone call, and they said, go ahead. I went to the phone booth near the door and I called my brother. I told him what was happening and he said like he said before, I shouldn't pay them, that I should stick to my rights. And that's exactly what I did.

" 'I'm not gonna pay off,' I told them again. 'The best thing you can do is give me a summons and get out of my store. I know my rights.'

" 'I told you, he's a wise cocksucker,' Repaci said."

In the street, meanwhile, Dexter Trotta was making his complaint. A headstrong boy, he wanted his pickle.

" 'My pickle, I want my pickle!' I told my father.

" 'Later,' he said, pulling me across the street.

" 'Please,' I said.

"Finally, my father stopped and he gave me a dime. So I went back in the store.

" 'What do you want?' one of the cops asked me.

" 'A pickle,' I said.

" 'Get out of here,' he said.

" 'Will you please let me take care of my customers?' Larry said.

" 'This kid a customer?'

"Larry said, 'Yes, he is.' "

" 'All right, give him his pickle,' the cop said.

"I put my dime on the counter and took the pickle. Then, it was scary, the cop swung his arm and knocked the whole pickle jar over. It fell on the floor with a crash and all the pickles spilled over everything.

" 'Now get out!' he hollered at me.

"I ran out of the store, and into the street, and I couldn't help it, I stood there watching. I could see through the window what was going on inside."

What he was to see was more horrifying than the "scary" experience inside.

"McCole went to the door after Dexter left and he locked it from the inside. It was just to scare me, I thought. I didn't care; I wasn't going to give in to them. And that's exactly what I told him.

" 'All right,' McCole said to me. 'I guess we've got to take you in.'

" 'Okay, take me in. But I'm not paying off.'

"I started walking along the counter to get to the other side when Repaci reached out and grabbed me like I was some kind of savage. They grabbed me and spun me around. I was pushed back against the counter, it was crazy, then they slammed me to the floor. I heard a crash as I went down, and a pickle jar hit the floor. The next thing I knew they were beating me, kicking me. They really kicked me—in the head. I tried to cover my head with my arms and they kicked me in the ribs. Then Repaci pulled out his pistol and started to hit me with it. McCole, he was holding me down and Repaci kept slugging me. Then there was blood. I could feel it running all over my face and head, I could see it on the floor, wet, red stuff mixed in with the pickle juice. I started to get dizzy, and Repaci, he kept slugging at me.

11

Then I heard McCole shout for him to stop. 'That's enough. That's enough!' he said, and then Repaci said, 'I oughta kill this black motherfucker,' and he slugged me some more.

"I could hardly see. Blood dripped into my eyes. The next thing I knew, they put the handcuffs on me, my hands behind my back, and they were dragging me to the door, my face along the floor. They squeezed the cuffs to the last notch. It felt like I couldn't get blood circulation. They dragged me into the street and shoved me into the squad car . . ."

From where he stood, young Dexter Trotta saw enough of this to send him scurrying across the street to 953 Lafayette Avenue, as fast as his bulky little body could take him, and he ran up- stairs hollering for his father.

"The cops, they were dragging Larry out of the store, and he was all bloody and they were kicking him. They took him around the corner to the police car on Stuyvesant Avenue and they hit him in the head as they pushed him into the car. When they got him inside, one foot was hanging out and one of the po- lice kicked at his foot, trying to get it inside. It was like he was dead already."

Bernard Trotta saw most of the action in the street, confirming his son's account. "When I heard Dexter, I came running out. Beverly Harris was with me. I saw them pulling Larry into the street like a sack of garbage, and I thought, I couldn't hardly see how they could've done it so quick. Like I said, they must've been waiting for me to get out of the store.

"It was pretty bad, all right. When I was in the store, I had a pretty good idea what Larry was talking about with the cops. I know what goes on in these parts. I mean, it happens all the time. Me, I work for Western Carpet, been there for seventeen years, but out in the streets it's all different. Larry, he was angry, all right. He didn't want to pay them anything and he said it over and over. I've known him for about two years, I guess, and I'd never seen him angry before. I guess the cops got sore at him then, but he wasn't doing anything, just standing there, talking, that's all. He didn't have any weapon or anything. He had his hands up there on the counter far as I could see. They had no right to beat him up like that. No right at all. He wasn't a crook. There was no numbers, no policy running from the store. He was just a nice guy trying to make a decent living. He wasn't even selling beer. No, sir, he couldn't have been making very much. He couldn't have been making very much at all."

"They drove me to the Precinct [the 79th Precinct station house] with the siren wailing like it was some big deal they were doing. At the Precinct, they pulled me out of the car like a rag doll, stood me up, a hand under each arm, and shoved me up the stairs like I was a monster who had just stuck up the First National Bank and shot the guards. They dragged me into the back room and pushed me against the wall. I was still hand-cuffed and bloody and my head hit against the back of a metal file cabinet and down I went again. I really thought I was a goner. They were going to kill me. I sincerely believed that.

"They threw me into a chair and put a bar between my arms and those handcuffs. And they hollered at me: 'What the hell is your name, you goddam nigger?' They were laughing at me, all the cops in the room, coming off duty, some of them. They kept saying to each other, I had thrown a pickle jar. I guess that was the story Repaci had started. 'Was it kosher pickles?' they laughed. Oh, man, they were really cracking up. 'You oughta know, nigger, you just can't beat City Hall,' and comments like that. Meanwhile, the blood was just pouring out of me, dripping down the side of my head, and I was getting real dizzy again."

When John Blutcher hung up after his brother's phone call, he hurried to finish a few chores, put on his winter jacket, and walked up Lafayette Avenue toward Stuyvesant.

"I got to the intersection at Sumner and right away I knew there was trouble. I could see the patrol car and a lot of people standing around. I hustled as fast as I could, but when I saw the car pull away, and then heard the siren wailing, I knew I was too late, whatever had happened.

"I found out quick enough. Bernard Trotta saw me coming and he told me everything. It was wild, all right. We went into the store, the whole thing was open, wide open. The cops had left it that way, not caring about the store. It was a mess. Stuff knocked over, potatoes rolling all around the floor, the slop of the pickle juice and the pickles, and blood. You could see the blood all over the place, all smeared up like they must have dragged him through his own blood. I said to Trotta, 'Don't touch anything,' and then we left, locking the place behind me.

"It didn't take long. It never does. There were about forty people around, and the word was spreading. You could feel the mood, you know the kind of mumbling that starts to grow. There was going to be trouble, all right, and I thought, dammit, maybe there ought to be. Trotta and I, we hopped a cab and went down to the Precinct over on Throop and Gates, and the next thing, there were all those people come over there, too. A crowd gathered outside the Precinct house. Forty, maybe more. There was a lot of yelling and cussing going on, but the police wouldn't let us in. Not even me, his brother. All they said was for us to relax, that everything was going to be all right. But no one was going to. A few of them started to collect rocks and bottles. Not just the young ones. Grown-ups. Some of them would close in on the cops who were coming in or out of the Precinct, cops who had nothing to do with the matter. You could tell they didn't know what the hell was going on. The brothers and sisters would surround them, close in on them and holler at them, nose to nose, holler in their faces about what kind of savages they were for beating up on Bubba. You could hear the voices from way away, louder and louder. It was like in the movies when the crowd gathers outside the sheriff's office, you know, when they want to take some poor nigger out of jail and lynch him—only this was the opposite.

14

"I felt like a violent man that day. I mean that, violent, and I'm not a violent man. It was the wrong time for it, though. It was in the air, the feeling that a lot of us would get hurt. I guess I got smart at that moment. I was full of cop hate, but I got smart. If I'd have done the wrong thing, I would have thrown away all my work with the organization. It would have folded up if I'd have gone violent. It would have ruined everything and nothing would have been gained. A man gets real mad at times, but he's got to learn to cool it. Instinct, I guess. I went around getting everyone to subside. I pulled them away and warned them to stop. I must have talked to half the people there, stopping them from doing something crazy. It was something to see, all right. Even the police looked scared. I could see how a riot can start. A thing like this. Most of the people hardly knew Bubba. But they knew the cops. They knew the 79th Precinct. And that was enough for them.

"The trouble was, the police had gone too far again. Over and over, they go too far. Especially here, in the 79th. When the people don't believe the police, when they don't trust what the police do, you don't have no more chance for law and order. The police are the ones that have to create the trust. If they go around beating up people like my brother, making false arrests, jumping all over the innocent ones, then nobody has a chance for peace. Nobody. I stood out there in the street, trying to get inside to see my brother, and all I could think was that they had gone too far. It would get so nobody would bother to separate right from wrong, innocent or guilty. The people would jump all over the police even if the victims were wrong. That destroys the whole community. But when things like this happen to Bubba, how could you blame the people?"

Inside the Precinct, the official police machinery of booking and arrest was being executed. McCole and Repaci submitted their reports. Repaci, however, was suffering from severe pain in his left thumb, afraid it might be broken in some way. When the ambulance arrived to take Blutcher to the hospital, he went with

15

it. McCole, too. It was, after all, part of their duty to bring their man into custody—in this case, to the prison ward of the hospital.

"The next thing I knew, I was in the ambulance, and they were taking me to the hospital. I looked up and saw McCole and Repaci, they were riding along with me. I was still handcuffed, and my wrists were hurting almost as bad as my head. I could feel them all puffed up from lack of circulation. I saw a black man in the ambulance, in a white coat and all, so I said to him: 'Look, these handcuffs are tight. Could you get them to loosen them?' But he shook his head, looking over at Repaci like he was more scared than I was. 'No, I can't do that,' he whispered. 'You just take it easy, boy,' he said.

"I thought, wow, the white cops beat on us because we're black, but there are still blacks who don't know enough to act like brothers."

Dizziness and pain enveloped him. He felt himself slipping into that gray area between consciousness and fainting. Blutcher resisted, struggling to keep his eyes open, terrified that if he failed, he would never open them again, until, gradually, it all became too much for him. He let out a feeble cry and then blacked out.

2

"When Larry was born, my husband went scootin' out of the house crying out to everyone, 'I got me a new baby boy!' But by the time he came back, he had a new baby girl, too. Oh, he screamed about that, but he didn't go outside again for fear of what might happen if he did. 'Woman,' he said to me, 'how many more babies you gonna give me?' I couldn't blame him. We'd been married for only seven years and there were four others chasing around . . .'"

Mrs. Epsie Blutcher was born in Lumpkin, Georgia, as were her parents and grandparents before her. So, too, was Earvin Blutcher, the father. Beyond them, the family tree is obscured by inadequate recall and the chaotic circumstances of Southern slavery. How many hundreds of years deep were the roots? How many generations of labor had they given to Georgia soil? "It goes back to forever," she said. "It was never any other way but working the land."

Larry's parents knew each other as teen-agers, as students in

Lumpkin Junior High School. The mother's people had land, accumulated through penny-saving and endless labor since abolition in 1865, a large piece of land to grow cotton, corn, peanuts, soybeans. (Her great-grandmother, Hannah Brown, died when she was over a hundred years old. She was bringing in a cow when it was frightened by a snake, and it jerked her so violently she was killed.) The father worked as a farmer—as his father had worked—but there was a restlessness in him that kept him unsettled. "He didn't have the feel of a farmer," Mrs. Blutcher said.

Lumpkin was a peaceful town, its population a steady 10,000, half white, half black. There were several black landowners. (The Blutchers were proud of their cousin, for example, a man who ran a 700-acre farm and a general store.) The Blutchers lived on the plantation of a white man named Horace Moton, and they share-cropped cotton and peanuts. Their home was a rickety frame house with two bedrooms, an outside water pump, and an adjacent outhouse.

"Life was not easy, but it was decent enough for the children, always outdoors and all." Mrs. Blutcher was a proud and vigorous woman, "I always did everything I had to do, and I did it myself. The family gave me happiness. I sure loved those children."

As with most farming families, there was always something to eat. "My father used to kill a hog once a year," John Blutcher remembered. "He'd kill it in November and it would last up to May or June. We'd smoke it so the meat would keep. We'd also have chicken. We always had chicken on Sunday."

"It wasn't too bad as I remember it," Larry's older brother Bill recalled. "I remember how we used to go over to the Moton place. He had a son named Ames. We'd go over there, about a half mile away, and they'd give us bread and honey. We'd take the honey right out of the beehive and chew on the beeswax."

School was taught in the Methodist Church, a two-mile walk, an old one-room building that serviced the Negro grades one through six, a man and a wife teaching all the subjects.

"You grew up real simple," Bill recalled. "Out-of-doors most of the time. You didn't have much in the way of clothes and gadgets, but then, neither did anyone else around except maybe some of the white folks. You play around, do some chores, go to school, and when you get old enough, you have to help with the farming. I remember helping with the mule. We had a mule named George, and my father used to swear at him to get him to move. We'd listen to him swear and it'd always make us laugh."

Seventy-two years before Larry was born, the blacks were slaves, growing the peanuts, cotton, corn, plowing the thick clayish Georgia soil behind a mule. They lived in ramshackle farmhouses with outside pumps and outhouses, dependent upon their white master whose kindness or cruelty was the primary determining factor in their security and happiness. Their culture was limited by that of the white master and their obeisance to him was the dominant ethic of their existence.

Seventy-two years after Emancipation, it had changed, but barely.

Three generations had passed since slavery, but time seemed to have stood still in the Lumpkin setting of Larry Blutcher's birth. Slavery was dead, but its death remained far more legal than factual. The free citizen named Earvin Blutcher spent his days behind the mule, lived in the same rickety home, ate no better food nor more of it, and had seen no more of the world than his dependence on a white master would permit. If he could boast of an education that had left him literate (he could read and write and knew something of white man's history), it had been of little use to him. He did not vote and seldom read the newspapers. What he heard on the radio was the white man's message and not designed for his betterment. His subservient blackness remained at the core of his existence. The mores of slavery were present in his social and family traditions. In addition to the right to marry, he had one major opportunity that distinguished him from his forebears: he was permitted to leave.

The Blutcher exodus began in 1940 when Larry was three.

When one of Larry's brothers took sick, there was no money for doctors, no jobs for money, and the boy died. Earvin Blutcher decided he'd had enough of George's stubborn rump and the torturous, endless battle with the soil. He picked up his family and moved some thirty miles away to Columbus.

Out of the frying pan and into the fire. Literally. Three weeks after their arrival, their house burned down in a billowing conflagration that spread down the block and destroyed four other houses in its path. If there was no personal injury, the Blutchers lost everything else they owned. They moved in with grandparents until they could get on their feet again.

Both parents worked at the cotton mill in town, making thread. Together they brought home $53 a week, working staggered shifts, he from 3 to 11 P.M., she from 11 P.M. to 9 A.M. "We spent our mornings together with the children," the mother recalled.

In Columbus, Larry went to the Radcliffe School and, like his brothers, thrilled to such city phenomena as a fire hydrant spraying out more water than he had ever imagined, what seemed like towering buildings of steel and concrete, and a thousand buses and cars hurtling side by side on streets teeming with people. And the whites. They weren't nearly as friendly as the Motons. "We used to go to the park sometimes to pick the berries and plums, and the white kids, when they saw us coming, they'd eat their fill, then wipe shit all over the fruit . . ."

There was a complexity about urban life, and the end of innocence came more quickly. "I became fully conscious of the difference in being black. It was rammed into you, one way or another, every day. It's an old story now, but it wasn't then. You had to be on your toes all the time. You were taught to have a built-in warning system as to how to act when you were in the presence of a white. In case you didn't learn it right, there's always a time when it gets beaten into you. That's what parents know best in the South. I remember the store, Mr. Meadow's store, where my father used to buy the groceries. One day my twin sister Tiny and me gathered up old bottles, a whole wagon-load of bottles, and we brought them into Mr. Meadow's store. We got six cents for the bottles which seemed like a lot of money and we bought three cookies each. We were laughing and feeling good as we walked back home, and then we met Mr. Meadow's granddaughter. She saw us laughing and eating the cookies, and I guess she didn't like that. She spit at me, right in the face, and then she called me a dirty nigger. Well, I didn't like that. So I slapped her. When Mr. Meadow found out, he was so raving mad he came down to our house and got my father and brought him back to the store. And my father had to beat me there at the store in front of that little white girl. He beat hell out of me so Mr. Meadow would continue to allow him to credit groceries. I was only four years old then. But I knew I didn't like being called a nigger. I'd been told at home, too, always to call the white man 'Yes, sir,' and all, and not to get into any trouble. They let you know where it's at, and a kid better not step over no boundaries. The line is drawn for you, straight as an arrow. It was drawn so sharp, you get beaten up by your own father when the white man scares him into it."

Three generations since slavery.

Two black psychiatrists, William Grier and Price Cobbs, wrote the same story in their book, *Black Rage*. "Throughout his life, at each critical point of development, the black boy is told to hold back, to constrict, to subvert and camouflage his normal masculinity. Male assertiveness becomes a forbidden fruit. . . . Under slavery, the black man was a psychologically emasculated and totally dependent human being. Times and conditions have changed, but the black men continue to exhibit the inhibitions and psychopathology that had their genesis in the slave experience. . . . During slavery the danger was real. A slave boy could not show too much aggression. The feelings of anger and frustration which channelled themselves into aggression had to be thwarted. If they were not, the boy would be little or no use as a slave. If any feelings . . . were expressed too strongly, then that slave was a threat, not only to himself and his master but the entire system as well. For that he would have to be killed."

Columbus was no joy for the Blutcher children, and least of all for the father. In 1942, it was a city with World War II written all over it, a soldier town, brimming with the tensions of a conglomeration of blacks, Northern whites, local crackers and their women, a whole city full of strangers, loose money, young prostitutes and more taverns than schools and churches combined. It was a town and a time that fed on the weaknesses of men, building up their frustrations, leaving them susceptible to the sweet talk that might conceivably better their lives. Wars have a way of upsetting the *status quo,* even with those who are fortunate enough not to have to fight them. It is something of a historical truism—albeit exaggerated—that wars either kill people or bring them affluence. To Earvin Blutcher, restless and malcontent, it didn't take much to get him moving. He had met a young Northern soldier in Columbus, a New Yorker friend of a distant cousin from Philadelphia, and he constantly talked about all the money a black man could make up in those big Eastern cities, especially now that there was a rising shortage of labor with all that war work going on. As Larry recalled it: "Even though he ate pretty good when he came to visit us, he used to tell my father 'this weren't no place for a human being.' He said, 'I'd rather be hungry up North than be full in the South.' "

It was the kind of talk that had been luring black men North since the time of slavery. Indeed, it was the seduction sustained through an entire century, feeding a mass migration that has proved unstoppable even today, changing the economy and sociology of the entire nation.

The pull was simply too great for Earvin Blutcher. One day, he packed a bag, said good-bye, and left.

If Epsie Blutcher, now alone with the five children, resented his departure, she understood it, for she nursed the very same dream. Larry was barely five years old at the time, but his memory leaps with the repeated daily references to it. It was as if there were no other goal in life, no other chance for happiness. The North was the Southern black man's symbol of paradise, his chance for the Promised Land. Epsie Blutcher took her children to church on Sundays and kept them devoutly Christian at home. The family was held together by the force of her devotion and relentless energy. She left the cotton mill and went to work as a maidservant to white families. The hours were that much better. They heard from Earvin occasionally—he was working at Reynolds Aluminum in Philadelphia—an affectionate note with a few dollars in it, whatever he could afford, missing them all, wanting to have them all together again. She had faith; she kept telling the children they would all be going North before long. Somehow they would get the money to go to the Promised Land.

Then one night, she woke from a tingling dream, a dream of such magnificent promise she felt she could taste its fruition. She had dreamed a number. 210. The three digits danced in her head with such power, she was absolutely certain they were ordained by some superior Being. 210, she told the children. She was going to play that number with every dime they could scrape together.

It came to ninety cents. Ninety cents on a single number, by far the largest sum she had ever gambled. "I've never had a feeling like that before or since. I waited through that day with my feet barely touching the ground, I was so sure I was going to win."

It was phenomenal; number 210 paid over six hundred dollars.

It was more money than the Blutcher family had ever seen. Thereupon, she packed their belongings and they piled into a bus, all six of them, and rolled their way eight hundred miles to Paradise.

The year was 1943. Paradise was the borough of Brooklyn, in the community known as Bedford-Stuyvesant.

23

3

According to geologists, Brooklyn stands on an island mass of rubble that was rolled down from the New England mountains by a huge glacier—a process that spanned many thousands of years, an ice pack so deep that not even Mount Washington barred its advance. It was rubble blessed by nature, however, and the area gradually ripened into rolling hills with exquisite vegetation.

Paumonak Island, the Indians called it, and they thought of it as a land of paradise. It was so rich with rambling streams of clean fresh water, of berries, wild fruits, of fish and clams and small wild game, there was little need to farm anything but corn. In 1609 Henry Hudson himself, viewing Breuklyn (as it was named by the Dutch) from the *Half Moon,* described it: "as pleasant with grass, flowers, and goodly trees as ever they had seen, and the savage inhabitants who thronged around in canoes curiously fashioned from single-hollowed trees were comely in form and friendly in disposition." And later: "The varied and picturesque scenery of these virgin wilds formed as fine a land as the foot of man can tread upon"—while the Island of Manhattan, on the other hand, was craggy and bare. The Dutch visited as traders with the Rockaways and the Kanarsies; then, some 300 years before the Blutchers arrived, they purchased from local Sachems a tract of land to enlarge the Breuklyn border into a hamlet that became known as Bedford. The Indians called it Maerckkaakwich. The price: "100 Guilders Seawant [$40 worth of sea shells]. Half a tun of strong beer. Two half tuns of good beer. Three guns, long barrels, with each a pound of powder and lead proportionable."

Immediately, the Dutch brought in slaves. Slavery, in fact, became a lucrative part of all Dutch shipping. By 1750, the mercantile value of a prime slave was something over $120, their strong bodies essential to the needs of local farmers. However, these relationships became a constant source of irritation in the area, building to several violent outbreaks as early as the mid-eighteenth century, a hundred years before Emancipation. It was to the credit of Breuklynites that the last public sale was said to be that of four slaves belonging to the widow of one Heltjic Rappelji in 1773. There were, at the time, 133 slaves in Breuklyn, owned by 62 different families.

If the plight of slaves in Breuklyn was more civilized than their cotton-picking counterparts, it was nonetheless circumscribed by a number of oppressive laws. They were, for example, forbidden to "run about on the Sabbath," or to meet in groups larger than four (indicating a constant fear of conspiracy), or to purchase or imbibe in liquors which, as with the Indians, they were considered incapable of handling. However, an Easter celebration was permitted them, as Henry R. Stiles records it: "It was their annual saturnalia. The village was black with them. They danced around the market, they sang, they tooted on fish horns, played practical jokes on one another; and, everywhere through the village might be heard the cackle of obstreporous laughter by which the negro is wont to give relief to his overplus of happiness. . . . As a necessary consequence, the negroes generally got as jolly drunk as lords, and on the following morning as many as 25 or 30 would usually be brought up before old Squire Nicholls on a charge of disorderly conduct who, appreciating the peculiar weaknesses of the negro character, always treated the culprits with leniency; and, summarily confiscating whatever funds remained in their pockets after their spree, dismissed them."

Two hundred years later, in this very same community, the descendants of slaves were paid by white real estate speculators to stage drunken brawls on the Sabbath to drive white homeowners from the area in the vicious process known as blockbusting.

Overall, however, the Bedford area in 1776 was a bucolic community that was a paradise to the Dutch, "a simple forest environed by a cluster of ancient low-browed homes that presented a scene of quiet beauty." The inevitable transition from Eden to urbanization was far more gradual than that of neighboring Manhattan. Though a short ferry ride away, Brookland (as the English came to call it) remained pastoral long after Manhattan became a city. As late as 1820, "from the Fulton Ferry slip with its horse boat, its one steam boat, and its rowboat accommodations with no bell save the resonant throat of the ferryboatman, the old country road straggled crookedly upward and backward, out through Bedford . . . and even to Montauk Point." But as Manhattan began to fill its limited area, thereby increasing real estate prices, New Yorkers began to ferry across the harbor to the more expansive greenery, and by mid-nineteenth century, Brooklyn showed the first signs of a commercial life of its own: factories, warehouses, and eventually the beginnings of a crime problem. By 1850, it became necessary to establish a regular police force, patterned after that of Manhattan.

There were, at that time, over a thousand recently liberated blacks, slavery having been abolished in New York in 1827. Their freedom was immediately limited to the inevitable squalor of the first Northern ghetto, a collection of dismal streets near the docks where they were herded in poverty to scrounge for sustenance, abused, hated, feared. Of the fourteen schools in Brooklyn, only one was available to them; and they received a far greater percentage of attention from the police.

But in the main, Brooklyn was looked upon as the "bedroom of Manhattan." The 1870s were marked by the construction of many magnificent homes, some of New York's wealthiest people settling in the Bedford area along stately tree-lined streets, their large brownstone mansions designed in the finest traditions of urban living. Nor did the construction of the Brooklyn Bridge in 1883, opening the door to a fresh influx from the crowded island, bring an intrusion upon this elegant tranquility, for thousands of sturdy and luxurious homes surrounded the rich, built by speculators to accommodate the new upper-middle-class families of successful second-generation Germans, Irish, and Italians. The only Negroes in the area were domestics, maids, liveried chauffeurs, living in smaller homes on the fringes of these exclusive neighborhoods. They were well paid. Their children went to school with the whites. They were well treated as long as they knew their place. It was, in effect, a perpetuation of the old master-slave relationship, Northern style. These blacks became the grandparents of many of the leading citizens of present-day Bedford-Stuyvesant.

It wasn't until the opening of the Williamsburgh Bridge that the character of the area began its fundamental change, the first migration beginning about 1907 with the displacement of Jews and Italians from Manhattan's Lower East Side. They filtered into the Bedford-Stuyvesant sections, finding whatever residences they could, immediately diminishing property values in the surrounding neighborhoods. In the 1930s, the Depression initiated another change, stripping many of the marginal streets of respectable middle-class status, and suddenly there were blacks finding an outlet for the expanding needs of their growing population. In 1930, there were fewer than 30,000 non-whites in the area: it was a figure that would multiply in fantastic geometric progressions over the next few decades.

It was inevitable that this great transition should begin with hard times. A speculator would smell out a potential drift, then immediately go to work to implement it for his own profits. Start with a few homeowners who could no longer afford to maintain high social standards, first dismissing their servants, then selling their houses. Cautiously, a smart operator would permit a desirable neighborhood to "disintegrate" as slowly as possible, keeping the supply-demand ratio high enough to work for him. He selected a few choice Negroes for certain blocks, moved them in, then began a campaign of insidious pressure, circulating handbills (delivered by Negroes) stating, "I have a buyer for your house." He even hired blacks to pursue investigations, visiting white homes with fabrications about Negroes who had just bought from him on nearby streets, embellishing it with tales about all the neighboring whites who were in the process of selling. Any ruse to effect this was used, from artfully contrived rumors to staged, black drunken brawls. The art of blockbusting preyed upon the sanctity and security of the home, upon a wellspring of bigotry—and a desire to sell when the selling was good. In time, no street could withstand the panic implicit in living beside a family of color. Even the cooler heads who resisted, struggling to remain in old family homes, were finally forced to leave, overwhelmed by the avarice of their own bankers who sometimes worked in collusion with black brokers.

The ghettoizing of the Bedford-Stuyvesant community began in earnest following the end of World War II, spurred by the tremendous wave of blacks fleeing from the economic and social inhumanities of the deep South. And since Harlem was bursting at the seams, they, too, came to Brooklyn. Negroes with money found assistance from brokers and bankers, subdividing the fine old mansions into multiple dwellings at swelling rentals. Throughout the fifties, they came by tens of thousands in what realtors called "the most sucker-ripe housing market in history" and formed the second largest ghetto in America. The colored population of Bedford-Stuyvesant jumped from 6 per cent in 1920 to over 65 per cent in 1957, a quarter of a million blacks, over half of whom were under thirty.

The prospects were, indeed, foreboding. The average income of these people was $1000 lower than in the rest of Brooklyn, half of them earning less than $3000 a year, a sparse 5 per cent making more than $5000. An extremely high TB and infant mortality rate followed, together with a frightening climb of venereal diseases. Over 90 per cent of its housing had been built before 1919, and over a third was officially classified as dilapidated, with inadequate bathroom facilities, woodburning stoves, and a rapidly swelling population of rats and roaches. In the five-square-mile polygon that shaped its boundaries, with avenues proudly named after famous generals and American Revolutionary heroes such as Throop, Gates, Kosciusko, and Lafayette, there were now over 100 saloons and 77 liquor stores. The community that was famous for stately churches had become the site for tacky store-front religions.

It is an obvious sociological truism that ugliness and poverty breed hopelessness. It is also inevitable that established authority knows no way to cope with the resulting turmoil except with repression. To a new arrival, his first contact with police is likely to be, at best, unfriendly. Too many recent arrivals from the South found themselves facing forces scarcely less hostile than the KKK.

It took three hundred and fifty years. Man had turned that idyllic garden, Maerckkaakwich, into a jungle.

4

Epsie Blutcher brought her five children to New York much like an immigrant family fleeing from the poverty and oppressions of nineteenth-century Europe. They moved into an attic owned by the mother of the soldier whose sweet talk had lured Earvin Blutcher north. It was a cold introduction to the Promised Land, especially after the warmth of Georgia, three small chilly rooms in a roach-ridden tenement, toilet facilities to be shared downstairs. The father kept his job in Philadelphia with the Reynolds Aluminum Company, and came visiting on weekends bearing wrapped-up rolls of nickels for the children. The mother found work as a domestic and struggled to maintain the optimism that had brought them there.

"I fretted and prayed. The more I fretted, the more I prayed. It was all so crowded, so busy, so noisy, and I didn't know how to make do. It was all for the children, this coming North, to give them a chance when they grew up. But it sure didn't seem like much of a chance."

After a few years, she found a better place to live at 686 Lexington Avenue, a few blocks away, between Reid and Stuyvesant. And time helped her adjustment. There were, after all, so many people in the same rocky boat.

"It wasn't so good and it wasn't so bad. Good jobs seemed to be impossible up North just like they were in Georgia. One thing, you had to work harder up North. Much faster. Everything was always on the go. Then, too, down there, you know where you stand with people. I could never get used to the way they treated you up here."

It was easier for the children. They adjusted to the streets and took their pleasures where they found them. Larry was small and wiry with a quick agile body and a curious mind. "We never had any money, so when we wanted to go for a ride, we used to sneak on the El. We had to climb over a high fence and walk the tracks to the station to catch the train. I remember when I first learned about the third rail: one of us kids tripped on it and almost got killed by the shock.

"We heard that you could pick fruits out at New Lots at the end of the line, so we went. It was something, all right, not at all like the city. More like the South. We went there quite a few times. There was a man we called Farmer Brown, rode a big brown horse. He was a mean old guy, kept trying to chase us off his land, to keep us from the green apples in his orchard. One time, Farmer Brown wasn't there, but some older white boys came chasing out and caught one of my friends. They tied him to a tree and used him for target practice, one boy throwing his knife into the tree as close to my friend's face as he could. He was a good knife-thrower, all right, but it scared us all half to death. We started throwing rocks to get him off. Then the knife pinched a piece of my friend's ear off. He started to bleed and they ran away. It was the blood that scared them, not the rocks. We cut my friend loose, and put a handkerchief over his bleeding ear and it stopped. We took off across New Lots, over big sand piles, down to a lake. It was dirty, lots of tin cans and dirty slime on top. We swam anyway, those who could, but when we got back to shore we discovered that our clothes were gone. The white boys had thrown them into the lake. The shirts and pants were floating, but not the shoes. The shoes were gone. We made our way back to the subway in sloppy wet clothes, wrapping our feet in newspapers and paper bags because of all the crud that was sticking to them. All those white people on the train stared at us. We were ashamed, but we laughed. I guess they thought we were a bunch of savages or something. We laughed because it had been a big adventure and now we were going home, safe and sound.

"But my mother saw the paper bags on my feet and all she cared about was that my shoes were gone. I got a big whopping for that. 'Your father and I work hard for your things. You've got to learn to take care of them.' Parents don't listen to reasons why you don't have your shoes. They don't care about reasons, they have to work so hard. They just work to buy you things and expect you to keep them. That's the trouble, I guess; nothing else matters to them."

At Public School 57, Larry was a fair student with commendable deportment. He learned basic skills in reading and writing but showed no great interest in his subjects. Only art intrigued him. He loved to draw and paint.

"One day I was walking to school and I found fifty cents, hid it in my back pocket. At lunch time, I bought a whole load of candy and gave it to everyone in the schoolyard, just as the bell was ringing, an old cow bell signaling us to return to classes. The trouble was, the kids wanted the candy so I got blamed. My teacher, Mrs. Rogers, punished me by sticking me under her desk while she taught the class. Well, that wasn't so bad. I spent the time looking up her dress.

"I was only about ten, but I fell in love with a little Italian girl named Vito. She had silky black hair and a cute little laugh. I tried real hard to make her like me, even to the point of getting a little too sassy with Mrs. Rogers. Next thing, I was called down to the principal's office and she sent me home with a note to my mother. I wondered what it said, but she didn't tell me. That night at dinner, she said to my father: 'Well, Earvin, I thought you might like to know we've got a new man in the house.' My father, his head snapped up: 'Who?' Mother pointed to me, and I ended up with my head between my father's legs, his belt smacking across my butt. It was a real thrashing and I'll never forget it. After that I didn't sass the teacher so quickly. Trouble was, it was all started because of a girl and *that* was a lesson I didn't learn so fast.

"Then, one day we were studying about Eskimos. Everyone had to draw an igloo. Well, I liked that. I drew the best igloo in the class and when Mrs. Rogers saw that, suddenly she began to take a real interest in me. I hadn't been doing so well, and my mother had come to see what ought to be done to help me along. It was crazy: she and Mrs. Rogers began by having an argument about me, but then, after the igloo, they became friends. Real friends. It was something special, all right; the white teacher visiting us at home, and once, she took us all to a restaurant. I'd never been to a restaurant before. The first time in my life I had egg salad. Wow, it was something. Mrs. Rogers was my good friend after that."

All the Blutcher children showed excellent deportment in school. Teachers, beset by a growing problem of class discipline, liked their respectful, polite manner. Epsie Blutcher had insisted on that. Larry's school records show the home as highly rated, an indication of the stability of the family unit. Indeed, it was a strict, well-structured, closely knit family. The Blutchers went to church together on Sundays, and the mother insisted on adherence to Christian principles. Punishment was freely doled out. There could be no progress with children without keeping tight reins on them. The premise was based on the elusiveness of survival itself: trouble was everywhere; a sudden unwary slip into the abyss could be brought on by a child who did not know how to deal with the world. If trouble was defeat, its avoidance was victory. The child who learned how to stay out of trouble would emerge a successful adult.

Epsie Blutcher preached to them out of her Bible and watched in fear of their departing from the docile traditions of the South. Southern blacks were shocked by the smart-alecky style of Northern kids, the way they sassed adults and baited authority, for such was the road to death and the devil himself. Yet to a boy like Larry, there was something tremendously appealing about it, for in its aggressiveness there was strength and defiance, a style that satisfied a fundamental craving in all young people groping for manhood.

It was inevitable, therefore, that young Larry would get caught in the cultural clash of home versus the streets. It was a testimonial to the power of his mother that all five children remained under her dominance for as long as they did, especially in the face of Bedford-Stuyvesant's rapidly shifting black-white ratio. The presence of whites in the community was always a force for restraint and control. If children were abused and pressured by their white classmates, they were also challenged to be at their best. However, the whites were leaving, moving across community borders into suburban developments, leaving the growing mass of blacks to face their ghetto alone.

"When I was a kid on Lexington Avenue, I never thought of poverty. Being poor was a way of life. It was just living, that's all, as natural as breathing, as walking on the streets, as the way we played and the things we did for kicks.

"There's different seasons for everything on Lexington Avenue. There's a time for the rug gun—a rubber band attached to a stick, with cut pieces of some old rug out of a back yard, and you shoot it like a slingshot. You always think of war when you play. War is the thing on Lexington Avenue. We were always fighting wars in the neighborhood. The older guys, they had real gangs. Gangs like the Dukes, the Apostles. They were stealing gangs, vicious gangs. You were told that you had to belong to a gang because if you didn't you'd get snuffed out.

"My mother never wanted us to go into a gang, so I stayed out. I stayed in the background. I knew the gangs were wrong because that's what they were always telling me in church. My mother always had us praying, saying blessings before we ate and all. We were taught to obey God and pray to Jesus who had no respect for gangs. But even though you're a Christian, you'd better belong to something to survive in the neighborhood. Mothers just don't know what goes on in the street. They're in a different set, all those women. They're thinking about how they can make it better for themselves and the kids like they tell it in the movies. Man, there's just some things those women didn't know . . ."

Earvin Blutcher had given up his Reynolds Aluminum job in Philadelphia. He was feeling ill and wanted to be with his family. He took a lower job at less money as a porter at a pocketbook company a few blocks from the apartment, and once again, as in Columbus, he and his wife worked at the same shop. As Larry remembers their apartment:

"It was a cold-water flat with a coal stove for heat, and the wind blew right through the place. I used to sleep with my two older brothers in a pull-out couch and, man, I hated to get out of bed. What saved me from freezing was those quilts my mother made. All in all, it was about the same way my friends lived. In the big families, with ten kids, say, they were on relief and the kids would have to go out and steal."

The Blutchers were always too proud to go take welfare money, and the children were severely disciplined never to steal.

"Most of the guys I knew went in and out of jail. As I grew older, you became more and more conscious of jail. What saved me was that my family went to church and I always had a sense against doing anything wrong. As the years went by, I'd see how others got into trouble. They'd hang out at a bar on the corner of Lexington and Reid with nothing to do all day, and the next thing, they'd make the switch from the bottle to the needle. Man, that's another thing. Those drugs. It would keep them on a hustle, and they'd spend all their time stealing to supply the habit.

I see some of them to this day, standing at the same corner, nodding away. They just nod, that's all . . .

"We had some good times, though. Like when we were kids and would get mickeys. Every day a white man named Jack would come down the block with his horse and wagon full of potatoes, and when we got some, we'd take them into the back yard and build a fire and cook them. We had an old shack we used to call our clubhouse. The girls would come back there and we'd take them in the shack and if we gave them a mickey, we could have relationships with them. Least, we always thought that's what it was. After all, we were only nine or ten years old.

"Actually, the first time I had a sex experience, I was five years old. It was with a fourteen-year-old girl who used to come to baby-sit. She unhooked my pants and reached her hand in and played with me, and then she pressed my penis on her vagina.

"When we were kids, the big thing was to discharge. If you could, you'd really feel like a man. That was the big achievement, all right. I remember how I used to hear about it all the time and I never could. I had the good feelings, but I couldn't get to discharge. No matter what I did, nothing worked for me. I mean, I was worried, like maybe there was something wrong with me. Then one night, it happened in a dream. I wasn't doing a thing but sleeping and dreaming, and it happened. That made me think what a strange thing was nature.

"As teen-agers, we all had relationships with quite a few girls. I mean, that's pretty much what all the guys thought about. We were lucky because that's pretty much what all the girls thought about, too. That and getting enough money to buy clothes. When you think about it now, seeing as how so many of us have become different types, we really were pretty stupid about everything. I mean, we didn't go anywhere or see anything outside the neighborhood. It was like the whole world was that neighborhood. Sure, you'd watch TV and sometimes you'd see something that would get you talking about Africa or the South or Rich White People, all the things you never see or think about much. But mostly, you live your life right there. It's your territory and you feel safe in it. You just don't bother to leave it, that's all. There are hundreds of guys who never even get across to Manhattan.

"I used to think, maybe things would've been better if we'd stayed in Georgia. There we had our own house with a lot in back. We were independent compared to this. It was a lot easier for everyone—or so it seemed. I could never understand why all the grown-ups had this big dream about coming North to find paradise."

The son saw it as the father lived it: Earvin Blutcher began to die well before his time, his body destroyed by what he considered to be the best job he ever had. As Larry had put it: "the chemicals had gotten to him." He developed respiratory ailments, then a mild heart attack.

"Still, he kept up his spirits. He was a funny man and everybody liked him. We used to sit around the coal stove in the apartment and he told us 'haint' stories. Ghost stories. He was a good storyteller. One story I remember, he told us a ghost story but it was supposed to be true. About a man who tried to kill his wife by making her eat to death. He roasted a whole hog and tried to make her eat the whole thing, and when she refused, he chopped her head off. He buried her in the back yard and took on another woman, a nice young thing—but the first one, she came back every night at midnight and banged on the shutters calling 'Whooooeee,' like the wind, until finally the man went crazy and had to kill himself.

"It was better than TV, sitting around like that with him."

During the early fifties, the last years of the Truman presidency and the war in Korea, Larry was a young teen-ager at Junior High School 129. He stayed primarily with three friends, forming a sort of buttress against the powerful gangs that dominated the socio-military life of the Bedford-Stuyvesant community. Third-generation Brooklynite Eddie Barnet was as heavy-set and dark-skinned as Leroy Taggert was lean and light, the latter a descendant of a mixed Indian-Negro heritage that lent a distinct flavor to his style. The third member of the group was a West Indian named Maurice Laurencian, a slight, fragile-looking youth with an extremely agile, probing mind and a dialogue rich with romantic patois. It was very nearly as disparate a foursome as could be joined, but the friends remained tight over all the years of their struggle to maturity.

"Larry was a very calm guy, never any kind of a troublemaker," Eddie recalls. "There were too many guys around who were the opposite and I guess I wanted to stay away from them. He was sort of serious. Very trustworthy. Once, we were all out cruising around and we ran into a bunch of kids we knew. One of them said, 'Let's snatch a pocketbook,' and Larry tried to pull me away. But this one guy, he was the leader—you know what I mean?—and damned if he doesn't grab some old white lady's bag right there on the street. We all start running, the lady is screaming her head off, the cops are blowing their whistles. All of a sudden, the guy throws the pocketbook at me. I catch it on the run, like a forward pass in football, so the cops grab me. I was sent to the Youth House on 12th Street. It was a terrible lesson for me, and since then, you can be sure I stayed out of trouble. My mother was really hurt by it. She was the head of the house, and I was the oldest son of eleven kids. One thing, though; she told me I should've stayed closer to Larry and it never would've happened."

They went to school together, grappled with math, geography, English, history, and increasingly nervous white teachers. They greased their hair in vain attempts to stimulate the white man's style, but only Leroy Taggert was successful, only because he didn't have to try. For Larry, it was the slightness of his body that troubled him most. He had seen a Tarzan movie and could not help but admire the actor's physique. He also saw a magazine ad relating to muscular self-development, and he induced his friends to join him at weight-lifting in the school gym. They stayed with this for years, especially Larry, who was most sensitive to his appearance as a physical man. Eventually, he scraped

39

together the money for his own set of weights, so intent was he on looking like a he-man.

"He would struggle with the bar bells long after the rest of us would quit," Leroy remembers. "He weighed less than I did, but he insisted on lifting heavier loads. That was the way he was, always very determined.

"I liked him especially because he came from a good family. He wouldn't make trouble and get me into trouble. He had good self-control. He wouldn't blow up. Things didn't seem to bother him that bothered me. Once, for example, a guy wanted to fight in school, just wanted to tear into Larry over some silly thing. But Larry was cool. He told him, let's talk it over. But the guy wouldn't, so Larry, still cool, says okay, we'd better go outside in the yard, and they had their fight out there. He just wouldn't provoke a fight, but he was able to handle himself pretty well."

The boys all worked on weekends and evenings after school. Larry had a bicycle and worked as a delivery boy for the Lewis Drugstore. It was a five-and-ten-cent job, as he put it—52 cents an hour. "We didn't get tips. That was the custom. One night, it was cold and raining, and I rode a long way to deliver some medicine to a lady [all the customers were white]. I was freezing and soaking. I didn't have any money and I thought I really deserved a tip. So I asked her, all very polite and all, but she slammed the door in my face. I felt bad. But I felt worse when I found out she called the drugstore and told my boss. When I got back, he bawled me out good."

He left the drugstore and got a job in Manhattan, delivery boy for the Accurate Messenger Service at 57th Street and Madison Avenue, where he made 75 cents an hour. "I saved the money to buy a graduation suit and to pay for my pictures and class ring. It was a difficult time for money in my family because my twin sister, Tiny, was also graduating and Vina was going to nursing school. My father had shifted jobs again and was working as a porter at the Miles Shoe Store in Brooklyn. The best thing about my new job was that I got to know Manhattan pretty good. It gave me a feeling that there was something else to see in the world. Every day when I went there by subway, it was like an adventure. . . ."

His friend Maurice, the West Indian, had more perceptive memories of Larry: "I was with Larry once, we were accosted by a gang of white boys, demanding our money. Out of fear, we gave. The fear was not in getting beat up, but of fighting white boys and then having his parents find out. The way they thought, it was all right to fight with other blacks if you had to, but never with whites. I could see Larry was squirming with the shame of his submission. He almost got sick from the shame, right there in the street. It was a worse defeat for him than getting beat up. His family had always put the pressure on him, since he was the youngest boy. His older brothers and sisters, they were all upward-looking, to be better than the lowest in the ghetto. What was sad, though, was that they didn't push him to be doing something right, something worthwhile, they just pulled to stop him from doing something wrong. What he needed was to do better in school so he would think of getting a good education, to go to college and all. But there was no tradition in the Blutcher family to accomplish this. One didn't have to learn anything; one just had to stay out of trouble. This, of course, was typical of Negro families all over, especially from the South. The mother and father both work. There is no time for studies and reading in the home until it is too late and then they just don't know how. The problem was to make a living. That was what the kids were taught to think about. Their duty was to go out and help the family, as soon as they were old enough. That was all that was expected of you."

Larry worked his way through public high school the way aspiring white youths work their way through college. He wanted that diploma. The family insisted on that.

"They tell me now that Boys High is really together. Well, that's something, all right. When I went there fifteen years ago, it was nothing like that."

When Blutcher graduated in 1955, it was a white-dominated school. Ten years before, Boys High School had been one of the finest academic secondary schools in the country. In mathematics, its traditions demanded top-level skills among eager students. Its graduating class sent boys to leading colleges in America, and from there into important positions in the arts, government, business, and the professions. On the walls of the trophy room, a large poster proclaims the names of its more illustrious alumni: Congressman Emanuel Celler. Attorney Louis Nizer. Composer Aaron Copland. Authors Isaac Azimov and Norman Mailer. The only black on the list was Tommy Davis, the baseball player.

Today, 98 per cent of the students are colored (23 per cent of whom are Puerto Rican) and barely 25 per cent of its graduates attempt to continue their education. Among the blacks, it was even worse at the time of Blutcher's graduation. For the first time, reading levels of ghetto-schooled youngsters had sunk lower than those who were refugees from the South. Only 10 per cent of blacks who graduated went on to college.

"I was around in those days," Dr. Norville Clark, former dock worker, physical education instructor, and Boys High's first Negro principal, recalls. "There were still so many whites around, I couldn't buy a house on this block. Now there isn't a white in sight."

Larry Blutcher's years in high school were not unpleasant nor were they any more inspiring than what had preceded them. He had tested slightly below normal in reading and arithmetic skills, his I.Q. was a low 83, and he was placed in a General Studies program as distinct from the demanding skills required of Academic Studies. He succeeded in passing all his courses except typing, managing an overall average of 72, performing far better in art and music than in English and social studies. He found ancient history fascinating and spent much time reading about that period.

His general conduct was co-operative and community-minded. He was appointed leader in such citizenship duties as the salute to the flag, service as lunch room supervisor; he worked in the Class Records Program and contributed his artistic talent on the Poster Club. He sang in the Glee Club and was an eager member of the gym team. His disciplinary record was excellent; he received only four pink slips during his three years for such minor infractions as tardiness or being humorously disruptive in class, and once for refusing to go to the office wearing a jacket. ("It was dirty and torn and I was sort of ashamed of it.") A significant indication of his interests could be found in the results of the Kuder Test, designed to evaluate preferences and inclinations. Here Larry rated in the 99th percentile in Social Service, 95th in the Artistic, 93rd in Musical—while, on the other hand, his interest in Mechanical was a low 35th.

He liked his years at Boys High. He felt a sense of participation in the bleak but tradition-scarred halls. He was able to mingle with white boys and even made a few friends. There were several white teachers who were friendly and helpful. He found that the thought of being associated with the white world on any level was gratifying to him. It was, as his mother had imagined it, the paradise part of their exodus from Georgia. To be treated as a human being, to sense that the school was as much yours as theirs, this was the stuff of dreams, and she looked upon it as an end in itself rather than an opportunity. She continued to insist that he obey and appreciate rather than question and learn. Her nightly concern not what he had learned but whether he had gotten into trouble.

Larry worked as hard as he could to measure up. He dressed neatly and kept himself clean. He chose the most responsible boys as friends. He made himself as pleasing to whites as possible, imitating their styles when with them, proud of whatever acceptance he could achieve. He continued to slap hot grease on his scalp in the ageless Negro process, as did most of his kinky-haired friends. Bedford-Stuyvesant was still a mixed community and Boys High School was still 60 per cent white. Those were the quiet years, the years before the storm.

"I don't recall any race incidents. I mean, we got along pretty good. Every once in a while there'd be a ruckus in the cafeteria at lunch, but no one ever thought it was really racial."

"The saddest thing of all is when a boy with his record does not do everything he can to continue his education," reported a guidance counselor at Boys High. "There were many colleges available to him. There are many more now. Community colleges with special night courses. State colleges. All he needed was the hunger. It is likely that if he had, he would have found some special area of interest, presumably in the arts, that would have helped him shape his future. The alternative—the scramble for menial jobs—inevitably leads to frustration."

It was his background, as his friend Maurice Laurencian had pointed out: there was no tradition to lead him in this direction. Upon graduation, Larry immediately threw himself into the job market.

Along with his friend, Leroy Taggert, he went to the New York State Employment Agency. There was nothing available for them, and it was suggested that they take a civil service test. But Larry's father was growing sicker and he needed work immediately. "A test takes a long time, I was told. A long time before you take it, and then another long while before you get placed." They heard that a hat factory on Flushing Avenue was hiring. "It was a beautiful office, clean and modern with nice pictures on the wall. We thought this was going to be a nice place to work. The foreman came out to interview us, and all he asked was to see our fists. We held out our hands and he chose me. I guess I had a bigger fist. Then he took me back in the factory, and wow, it was like a madhouse. Maybe fifty colored and Puerto Ricans jumping back and forth from one machine to another. Each man was working two machines. The foreman showed me how to press one felt hat down at one machine, then jump to another to work on that one, keep going, all day, all week, all for $48. I guess I wasn't very good at it, because he kept coming back to holler at me, how rotten I was. He hollered at everyone, but especially at me, pretty soon everybody was looking at me like I was a special criminal because I was getting him so sore.

"I didn't want a job like that. At the end of the day I told him so. I asked him for my day's pay, but he told me to come back tomorrow. We had a little argument about that, but he wouldn't give me the money. Tomorrow, he kept saying. Why not now? I kept asking. Naturally, he won. I came back the next day, but he was too busy to see me. Sure."

Larry then got a job at the Jubilee Lamp Shade Company, taking boxes off the chute. This time the foreman was friendly. "He'd come around and tell me jokes, make me laugh. It was all very promising—and then I found out—he was a queer. He propositioned me after two months, told me that if I was 'co-operative' he'd take care of me, he'd get me a raise and a responsible permanent job. Wow, I didn't want that kind of a deal either."

In leaving, he was left with nothing. He was eighteen years old and he needed a focus. He needed a place to be where he could work and be wanted for what he could contribute. He needed a job where he could give something of himself, something real besides his time. He went asking around and found nothing. He couldn't even find a friend who could do any better than he. The only advice he heard was that the United States Army wanted him. In fact, they were preparing to demand him.

"I thought, what the heck, I might as well go."

5

To the eighteen-year-old Laurence Blutcher, his career in the Army was an extension of his aimlessness. He fought no wars, not even internal ones. He saw nothing of the world overseas and little of America. He learned no lessons in the nature of man or the conflicts of society, and made no progress in the evolution of his self. It was, in effect, a barely memorable experience, as vapid and fruitless and uninspired as a hitch in the service is designed to be.

"Like my brother Bill says, 'You get three hots and a cot.' You're supposed to be satisfied with that."

He was content to go along with it, his youthful style relaxed with the abandonment of any responsibilities. He was in company with a million of his peers, black and white, supposedly representing the heartland of America, a community of young men with nothing to do but take orders. He took them. It was easy to submit to authority when everyone else was sharing it with you. It was equally easy to let your thoughts wallow in the frivolousness of barracks camaraderie wherein all of life is an endless chain of dirty jokes interspersed with a few rounds of bitching, just to prove to yourself that you're still a man.

He took his basic training at Fort Dix, New Jersey, then was shipped south to Fort Bragg. If the Army was integrated, Fayetteville, North Carolina, was not. On his first pass, Larry entered a restaurant with his black and white GI friends, drawn by the neon lights of its illustrious name, "The New Yorker," only to discover that local traditions did not permit them to sit together. "In fact, they wouldn't serve us at the black table for a long time, and when they did, the food was cold and rotten." It was not surprising that none of his friends did anything about it, even to the point of making comment. Larry was South again.

As a soldier, he was assigned to the 456th Field Artillery, but found it uninteresting. When he learned there was an opening in the kitchen for a baker, he jumped at it, drawn to a work schedule that gave him one day on, two days off. From this, he cultivated a rudimentary knowledge of baking and, in time, an intimacy with the black women of Fayetteville.

"That's what I remember best about the Army, my social life. First there was this girl, she was about thirty-five or so, and I was only nineteen. I met her on the street and we got to talking and the next thing, we went to this hotel together. We were in bed having relations when the cop broke in and pulled out his pistol. He said: 'Okay, you're under arrest, both of you.' He took us down to the Precinct where they pulled her aside, and I saw them talking to her. They let her go, all right, but they booked me. They took a mug shot, fingerprints, the works, then they locked me up overnight. First time I was ever in jail though I was too scared to ask why. There was even a write-up about it in the Fayetteville newspapers the next day. They put everything in the papers down there. Then they let me out the next day, never told me anything, just let me go. It didn't even cost me. I heard that the cop knew her, knew who her husband was and everything. She was the type who just wanted to have a good time and everyone knew it. A loose woman, all right.

"Then I met another girl in town, and she had a house, a whole big house, and she was paying only $24 a month rent. She had another girl living with her, so me and a friend, we paid the rent there. It was an A-number-one deal. I spent practically my whole time out there with her. But the trouble was, she had eight kids and she was looking for a husband. She was only twenty-nine years old and she had eight kids who were living out in the country with her aunt or something. She wanted me to marry her, she insisted on that, so I said, okay, I'll marry you, anything so she wouldn't throw me out. Well, when I got my leave to go home, I headed straight for the train station and never even said good-bye.

"I know, it was a rotten thing to do, after promising her and all. But a man has to do something down there. A girl like that, she's very scarce in town, what with so many soldiers. I had to hang on to that woman for as long as I could, even though I didn't love her or anything. I mean, sometimes a guy will do anything in the Army . . ."

"Anything" took him from the $24-a-month house to 15,000 feet in the air. Larry transferred to the paratroopers, for no other reason than that he was bored. "Sure, it was scary, I tell you that. My first jump, I looked back in the eyes of a white soldier behind me and his eyes were like glass. Everybody was afraid. It was funny, the first and second times I jumped, it was all right. But about the fourth jump, I got nervous. I don't know why, but I felt something was going to happen. Then, you know, my chute didn't open. I was spinning through the air, looking at the earth coming up at me, and I let go in my pants. Scared to death, I pulled my reserve, thinking that wasn't going to open either, but then they both opened. Wow, that was a rough scene, though. You think, this is it, the end, there ain't gonna be no more. You never know when it's going to happen. There was a guy who was killed in the class before me, for instance. Everybody kept talking about him. Then, you might get caught in a bad wind and land in the trees where you get yourself all scraped up, busted legs and all. It happens, it happens.

"But then, there's a moment or two after your chute opens and you're floating down in air and it's not too bad. You see your buddies all around you and the earth is floating up at you. It's pleasant.

"I got along all right. The 83rd Airborne used to be a segregated outfit, but there was a big race fight before I got there, and they integrated as a result. The officers were mostly white, the noncoms mostly black. I had a black company commander for a while, but he didn't stay very long. I'd say it worked out pretty well. It was like Boys High. You know, a few skirmishes here and there, but nothing serious. I just wanted to get through without trouble, so I did what they told me to do, even though some of it was just too stupid to believe. But that's the Army. You have to do it, stupid or not. I guess they give you stupid orders just to show you that you have to do everything whether you like it or not. Well, I did it and kept my mouth shut. I wanted to get an honorable discharge. Sometimes you think it's crazy and you get to wondering, why, why? Like the way they make you dig a hole, just to make you fill it up again. All day long, hotter than hell, digging and filling with no kidding around and some dumb bastard noncom hollering at you. You know there's no good reason for it, just some officer trying to make you feel like a rotten dog, to beat you down a little more. They *want* you to feel stupid.

"The Army. What can you say about the Army? Mostly, I suppose that it lasted three years and I got out with an honorable discharge. It was during peacetime and I've got to be thankful for that. Three years, and no one took a shot at me. Only thing, it was not so peaceful for me when I became a civilian again."

He was twenty-one when he got out of the service. He had no skills, no direction, no specific goals. He was back in the slums of

Bedford-Stuyvesant, after three years, far more ghettoized than before. His brothers and sisters were married, occupied with jobs and families. It exacerbated his own restlessness, especially since he didn't even have a girl. He was, in effect, back where he'd left off, sensing that somehow, in some very significant way, he had failed himself.

The day after he returned, he went looking for work. The New York State Employment Service could give him no help. Once again, they suggested he take a civil service test, but could not promise any jobs. It was 1958 and a recession had hit the economy; jobs were scarce and the civil service was swamped. Nonetheless, it would seem that taking the test should have been obligatory, regardless of immediate prospects. His failure to do so was probably more closely related to his fear of not doing well on it than the state of the current job market. He had never found comfort in his performance with the written word.

"I went to Brill's, a commercial agency on 42nd Street in Manhattan. I guess there are a hundred of those agencies around. They sent me to the Technicolor Corporation, where they started me off at $45 a week, working in the Receiving Department along with a Puerto Rican. We received everything that came into the place. We hauled it off the street and into the elevator, up to the fifth floor. Then back down to the street, start all over again. That was it. Every day, the same thing, hauling crates and boxes. Most of the time, I didn't know what was in them, and after a while, I didn't care."

He lived at home and gave his mother $15 a week. His father was sick and his mother was harassed, unable to make ends meet. She needed more money from her son, pressuring him repeatedly with the sting of her anxieties. To Larry, it was an equally dismal period of drudgery and overall frustration at an age when his juices were flowing at maximum. He didn't want to face the problems at home. He was far too restless for that. He would come home from work, change his clothes and go out. Get dressed up and hang around—street corners, candy stores, beer taverns—it didn't matter. Money was always on his mind, especially since he had to work so hard for the little he made. He was always conscious of his dress and the neatness of his appearance, and spent far more money on clothes than he should have. His laundry bill, for example, ran to almost 15 per cent of his salary, yet it was vital to him to put on a clean shirt every time he went out of the house.

He knew one thing: he needed a woman.

"Her name was Carolyn Miles. She was a beautiful girl. As soon as I saw her I wanted to meet her. It was the way she was standing there, still and straight, looking so soft and gentle. Her eyes were kind. When she saw me looking, she smiled a kind smile, not like the bitchy type. It was like her heart was smiling. Wow, I thought. When I went up to her my knees were shaking. I swear, I'd never felt that before. I introduced myself and she told me her name, and then I thought, I'd never known anyone named Carolyn before. And the way she said her name—it made me feel like jelly. It was all so honeylike and nice, I felt like I'd fallen to sleep on a floating cloud. I mean, I was really grabbed.

"We started going together. We'd take walks and hold hands and talk. I'd tell her about the Army and all, and we'd laugh together. It was crazy because I wasn't trying to be funny or anything. I was telling it like it was, but with her, it seemed to come out without any madness. Or she would feel so sad for me, I thought I must've been laying it on too thick. It was like I'd never really talked to a girl before, not without a lot of sweet talk and put on. With Carolyn, I just didn't. If I told a lie or made up some exaggeration, right away I'd feel silly. I'd pull it back. And then I'd tell it straight.

"It didn't take me long, I fell in love with her. It was beautiful, all right. I'd go to work at Technicolor in New York, and I wouldn't see a thing all day. I mean, I'd do my work. I'd work hard, lugging those crates and all, but I'd be seeing her face and those soft eyes would be looking back at me, and I'd keep hearing her name the way she had said it to me.

"And then she loved me, too. I was sure of that. So it followed that we would have relationships together. It was just natural that we do. We had them many times, here and there, wherever we could go that was quiet and no one was around. We loved each other and we wanted each other and it was good. It was very good and I'd never been so happy in my life.

"And then she became pregnant.

"It had never happened to me before, not that I knew of, anyway. It shook me up, all right. I mean, I just didn't know what to think. Everything was different all of a sudden. Like I'd be moving those damn crates and I'd break out into a big sweat. Man, I'd never done that before. Not like that. Not with cold sweat, anyway. I'd wake up in the middle of the night, and I'd be sick and my head would be spinning. It scared me. I was only twenty-one years old, but I guess I must've felt more like twelve. I just wasn't ready for it.

"Then she came out with it: she wanted to get married. She was nineteen but all of a sudden she seemed like thirty to me. She told me she didn't want to be a mother without being a wife, and she expected me to do what I had to do.

"Well, I just couldn't. I was making very little money and I didn't want to get married. I couldn't think of myself as being married. It seemed like it was only a few weeks before, I was soldiering at Fort Bragg, jumping out of airplanes and floating down to earth waving at my buddies, and here I was getting trapped into something I wasn't ready for. I was a coward, all right. I just couldn't help it. I told her no.

"If the pregnant business shook me up, my telling her no shook her up twice as much. She was staying with her mother and the both of them didn't like it one bit. At first, they would talk about it a lot, thinking maybe I would change my mind. We'd have arguments and all, and when you have enough of them, the bad feeling begins to sneak in. It got so I didn't like to go over there so much. I'd be working hard and I'd be very tired and I'd go home instead. And then when I'd see her, there'd be more arguments. Seems like we was arguing more than we were loving.

"One night, I was over in my brother John's place, an after-hours place he was running. I was having a beer and I met a girl named Carrie Jones. I was feeling pretty bad at the time and she saw that. She tried to cheer me up. She must have been pretty sweet, all right, because she got me going. We went out after a while, and then I took her home where she showed me her baby. She said she was nineteen too and that she'd had a baby from a soldier a year ago. She looked good to me, all right. I guess, maybe, I thought I needed a change of scenery because I started seeing her. And then I started to have relationships with her every now and then. I didn't think much of it. It was like something you do when you've got nothing better to do.

"Then one day she started looking sad. I saw that. I'd spend some time with her and she'd seem like she was ready to cry all the time. I thought, well, she'd found out about Carolyn and me, and that she didn't like that, that I was spending so much time with another girl. But I didn't say anything because I didn't know for sure. Well, one day I was home, I get a message that Carrie wanted to see me, that it was very important. So I went down to Jefferson Avenue where she lived and she was there, sitting on the stoop in front of her house. And the next thing you know, she tells me that she's pregnant.

"Wow, it was a double-header! Two in one year.

"Well, I didn't see much of Carrie Jones after that. I heard that she was going away, to upstate New York where she had relatives. But then, one night I got a call from her. It was a really grubby scene because Carolyn was with me at the moment, and *she* was very large at the time, maybe seven or eight months. She sensed something when she heard me talking to Carrie and she sure got frantic. But after a while, I calmed her down, and then I went down to Madison and Patchen Avenue to meet Carrie. But she wasn't there. I waited around for a while, but she didn't show. I figured, well, it couldn't have been too important after all, so I left. But then, two months later, two policemen came to the door. It was a Saturday morning and I wasn't home, but my sister Vina spoke with them. They were nice and calm, she said, and all they told her was that would I drop over at the Precinct, it had something to do with Carrie Jones.

"It sounded like nothing too much, and Vina told me I ought to go, so I went, thinking it was the right thing to do. I went on Monday and the detective, he acted real nice to me, too. I mean, he was real friendly and all, and I was relieved. We kidded around for a while and I was enjoying myself, right there at the Precinct. He started asking me questions about Carrie and me. I told him everything, very straight. Yes, I knew her, and yes, I had relationships with her. I didn't know what it was all about, but I started suspecting it had to do with the support of the child.

"When he finished, he wrote out a form and asked me to sign it, which I did. Then he got up from his chair and sprung it on me: 'You are charged with statutory rape. A felony.' He was smiling no more, you can be sure of that. No more of the friendly jazz. He just grabbed me by the arm and shoved me in jail. Just like that!

"It turned out that Carrie had lied to me. She was only seventeen. But how was I to know? They set bail at $1500, but you can get out for $75. Twenty-five for every $500. My father had to borrow the money. I was still working at Technicolor and spoke to a lawyer up on Madison Avenue, but he wanted to charge me $350 to handle the case. I was only bringing home $42 a week and didn't see how I could afford to pay that much. Then I talked it over with a friend of mine who'd been in trouble a few times, and he told me about a lawyer in Brooklyn named Ethel Mott, a black woman. I went to see her and explained it all and she agreed to take the case for $175.

"It was my first run-in with the courts and it was a nightmare. You keep getting called back and nothing happens. It took months, and I lost so much time from work, it ended up, I got

---

55

fired from my job. That's the way it happens. You can't hold on to a job when the courts are after you. You get the notice to appear, so you appear. That's the law. Maybe the other people in the case don't make it, or something gets stalled, some technicality delays the case, but you're there, just like they ordered you. You're there in the courthouse, and you're not at your job. So you get fired and the case just drags on.

"Mrs. Mott, she advised me that there was a way I could get out of this and not have any mark on my record: I had to marry Carrie. The charges would be dropped and I'd still be clean. She told me how important it was for a boy like me not to have a criminal record. Sure, I knew that. I was twenty-one years old and I was perfectly clean and I intended to keep it that way. But to marry Carrie Jones?

"It may sound crazy, but I decided that maybe I would. I was all in fear about it. I was still with Carolyn, the one I really should marry, but here I was thinking about marrying Carrie, just to keep from getting a police record. I just wasn't much of a man, that's all. I came close to doing it, all right: I went over to see her, I was actually going to ask her to marry me, or so I thought. But she was out, they told me, she'd be back in an hour or so. I sort of hung around the stoop waiting and this guy came up to me. When he heard I was waiting for Carrie, we started talking, and man, he told me plenty. He told me that the father of her first baby wasn't a soldier at all, but that he lived up the block all the time. He told me I was being tricked. Carrie was really a big liar. Oh, I checked on that, all right, and he was telling the truth. I got out of there real fast. Man, I took off like the wind. I wasn't going to marry anyone like that, whatever else happened to me!

"The trouble was, it didn't make any difference to the judge. Mrs. Mott, she plead for me, but the best she could get was a charge of attempted assault. That's what went down in my record. Rape reduced to attempted assault. Say it out loud and it sounds like I really went ape or something. I received a thirty-day suspended sentence, and from then on, I was a man with a mark on him.

"It was a sad day. My mother, it just about tore her apart. I could see how she was screwing up her face to keep from crying. She could hardly talk, her sadness stuck in her throat like she'd swallowed an apple whole. My father, he just shook his head, over and over, all day long. They didn't say nothing, blaming me or anything; it was just that no one in the family had that happen to them. Now they were afraid of what was going to happen to me, like I was going to become like all the others in Bedford-Stuyvesant, a criminal of some kind. We sat around the house and nobody said a word. You'd think someone had died. When we started talking again, you can be sure it wasn't about me or the case. Nobody ever talked about it again.

"Later, I met up with a social worker up in Manhattan, and she was investigating the matter. She asked me if the baby was mine. Hell, Carrie had named it Laurence Blutcher, Jr. But I said no. I denied the baby. I told myself I wasn't going to get tricked or anything. I felt I'd have to pay out a lot of money for support and I had too many hangups for that. But the truth was, like I said, I wasn't a man. I just wanted to deny everything. I couldn't think about my own child. All I could think of was that money going out of my pocket. I thought maybe the social worker believed me. She said she'd be getting in touch with me before long to tell me what they'd decided. Another load on my back. Something else to sweat over. Wow, it was getting tougher all the time.

"Meanwhile, I was still with Carolyn and she had a baby girl. We named it Gail, and she was a beautiful thing. Carolyn still wanted me to marry her, but I just couldn't. I didn't have any money, for one thing. I didn't even have a job, since I was fired from Technicolor for having lost so much time going back to court so many times. That was something, all right. I had worked there almost three years; I worked hard, and after the second year, I asked for a raise, but all they gave me was an extra two dollars a week. Then, when I get in trouble, they don't care what it's all about. Not interested. If you don't show up, out you go. I looked around for another job, but it was more of the same. Lousy work, lousy money. I didn't know what to do. My pop was getting sicker and my mother was getting down on me. I was getting desperate. Then I met this cat at the after-hours place and he tells me how I can make good money taking numbers. 'What the hell,' he says to me, 'you got nothing much to lose any more.' It was like the devil giving you all those good reasons for playing his game. Besides, I could add a few of my own. I mean, the numbers had been good to us, hadn't they? Old number 210 that brought us to the Promised Land from Georgia?

"I started taking numbers. Nickels and dimes, dimes and quarters. It was a lot better than some lousy job at lousy pay. Or so I thought. What happened was I had to take too many bets on credit. Everybody does everything on credit in the neighborhood. Sometimes it seems like there isn't a cool nickel in the whole damn neighborhood. So my book became short and I'd spend all my time trying to collect from people and that's about as low a job as anyone could think up, the devil himself couldn't work it any better. It comes out that I was always in the hole, and the next thing you know, I was taking numbers in the day and shooting crap at night.

"It was a bad life. You don't feel good about yourself. You sweat out every roll of the dice and your mind gets weary of it. You get so you don't know what money is any more. You lose all respect for money. You spend all those years working for money, learning how hard it is to make it, counting your dollars as payment for what you do as a worker. But when you start living by the dice, all that becomes nothing. That two dollar raise becomes a rotten joke. The $48 a week becomes a rotten joke. You're rolling those cubes and one moment you're rolling two dollars and the next, you're rolling a hundred dollars. It all blends into one. It don't matter how much you're rolling, it's all the same to you. You just don't care any more, that's what happens to you. You win, you lose. You feel fine when you win, you feel rotten when you lose. But all the time you know that it doesn't much matter any more.

"What was so crazy about my life was that I had to quit working the numbers, I just couldn't get my book straight, trying to collect on all that credit. My book was always short. They told me I couldn't handle it right and I was through. What was so crazy about it was that a few weeks later, I was sitting with my father going over the leads, single-action numbers (everybody in the neighborhood played single action), and we had a bunch of numbers listed on a piece of paper. It was like doping the horses, you figure out what's a good number to play. I was on my way out, and opening the door, a man pushes his way in, a guy I'd never seen before. He jumps on me and knocks me to the floor, then he grabs me like he wanted to kill me. We wrestled, and I finally got the upper hand and started to choke him. Like I said, it was crazy. I didn't know what it was all about, this strange guy in our house. A black man, too. Finally, he manages to cry out, 'Police! I'm police!' and my father, he panicked, shouted at me to let him up. So I do. And as soon as I do, he pulls out his revolver and stands there shaking, and I'm looking into the barrel, shaking too. He says to me, 'You're under arrest. Your name Bob E. Apt?' I said no, you've got the wrong guy. Then he sees the pad on the table, the work sheet for the numbers, and he grabs it, shouting 'Policy!' like this was a treasure of some kind. 'You're under arrest for policy.' I tell him, 'But I'm not Bob E. Apt.' He says, 'That don't matter. I've got to take someone down and it might as well be you.' He even laughed when he said it, it sounded so crazy. My father pleaded with him not to take me, explaining that we weren't taking numbers, that there was no law against playing them, was there? But he said he had to. He even wanted to take my father in. But I told him not to, that I'd go along. My father was having heart trouble and there was no reason to take us both in.

"He took me down to the Precinct on Bergen Street. They fingerprinted me, took mug shots, the works. Then they took me to Centre Street in Manhattan and booked me. From there I was taken to night court, it took all that time since the arrest. They set bail at a hundred dollars. Two weeks later I appeared in court and was fined $250. Violation of Penal Law 975: Policy. My father had to go out and borrow all that money to keep me out of thirty days in jail. I guess the man named Bob E. Apt has me to be thankful for. If there *is* such a man. I never did find out. All I knew for sure was that now I had two notches on my arrest record. It didn't matter much. At least it didn't seem to. Once you lose your cherry, it's all pretty much the same.

"Only thing, it was becoming a little too much for Carolyn. Gail was no longer a baby. She was two years old. And Carolyn was getting tired of the set up. It was the old problem. I should marry her. She wanted to get married for Gail, and I just couldn't. All of a sudden, she and her mother decided to move to Philadelphia. She decided that the best thing she could do was forget about me, to start a new life. I couldn't support her or the child, couldn't buy the things I should buy for the baby and all, and so they just up and left.

"I woke up one morning, I don't know, maybe a few weeks later, and realized how I missed her. It started to grow inside me that I loved her a lot more than I thought. I started to think, wow, what had I done. She was gone. My lovely little daughter was gone. I was a failure and a fool, and I hadn't done the right thing. It grew in my mind until I couldn't think of anything else. I decided I'd better do something to straighten out my life, at least to give it a try. But all I could think of was to go down to the State Employment office and tell them I wanted to take the civil service test. And then I started to think that it would be best if I did marry Carolyn. In fact, I knew that I really wanted to, I missed them so much. So I called her in Philadelphia. I called her and told her I wanted to marry her, and damned if she didn't turn me down.

"I couldn't believe it. I mean, in my mind, I had twisted and turned everything around and finally, I wanted to marry her, and then she said no. I went down to visit her, bringing presents for Gail and all. I played with the baby all afternoon, feeling all warm inside, loving them so, and I kept waiting for the night-time when Gail would go to sleep, wanting to be with Carolyn alone. Then about eight o'clock, she started to get dressed up, and I didn't know whether to be happy or sad. I asked her if she was going anywhere, and she said she wasn't. So I asked her to go out with me and she said no. And then a few minutes later there was a knock on the door and a man came in. All dressed up in slick neat clothes. I could tell, he was her beau.

"I walked down the stairs and my heart was so heavy I thought it would fall out of my body.

"I couldn't sleep, I couldn't eat, I could hardly breathe. I couldn't wait to get to see her again, to see if I could straighten the whole thing out, somehow to get her back. And the next day, there I was. When she saw me, she got frightened. She thought I was going to abuse her, and I explained that I would never do that, that I truly loved her and wanted to marry her. But she said no again. There had been too many hard times and she didn't want me any more. I was too late.

"So I left. I walked the streets, as lonely as a man could be. I bought a bottle of whiskey and drank a whole pint. I walked into a crap game and blew the $35 I had left. I felt like the whole damn world had ended. I wanted to die. I wanted to forget about everything and die.

"I didn't die. What I did was the opposite. I wanted to show her. I saved my money and bought Gail clothes. Over and over, I tried to impress Carolyn with how good I was doing, how I could support them, how we should be together because of our daughter. But she didn't see it that way. She didn't think that I had changed and was doing what a man should do. I kept on visiting and taking Gail out. We'd go out to the parks and go to the zoo and all, and it would keep on breaking my heart. One day Gail asked me: 'Daddy, why aren't you and mommy together like it used to be?' and I could hardly speak to answer. What could I say? What hurt the most was that I knew it was all my fault. All I could tell her was that sometimes things happened between grown-ups and that when she grew up she would understand.

"I would visit her at school to see how she was doing, and I'd send her Christmas presents and all, but it was no use. The years rolled by and it all began to fade. Finally, her mother sent her South. (That was in 1967.) I haven't seen either of them since. I spent a lot of nights thinking about them, about my life, about my daughter, and mostly about the mother of my daughter. I thought, wow, what a fool I've been. It's all really something, though. When you look back on it and you know that you've changed because you've seen how you've learned from what you've done, then it's all not so bad."

Larry had spent his young twenties in a continuing cycle of job scrambling, crap games, women troubles, and emptiness. He was twenty-five when his father suffered his third heart attack and died. He watched them bury the worn-out body knowing how hard the man had worked, how compliant he had been, how legitimate, always legitimate, how conscious of the white man's restrictions. He saw what every black man who plays by the rules sees clearly enough, that for all the struggle, there is no power. You go nowhere. There is no other way to go but nowhere. You work at your job and take what is given you. When luck is with you, the white man's economy keeps you working, and when it goes against you, you pull in your belt and wait until another door opens to let you in again. Meanwhile, you take a few nickels and put them on a number. Every day, a new day and a new hope. You keep on dreaming a number—everybody knows somebody who dreamed one right, or so they tell—and you play and pray. God will decide but the policy lords will prosper. That was the whole game and, like his father, you're not supposed to complain, you just suffer and die, for that was the Christian way, all inspired by the white man's God in His infinite wisdom.

Larry loved his mother, but he was growing away from her. She was all Christian, a true believer, and he was finding that a hard thing to accept. He was young and fumbling with the ways of thinking, but when she challenged him, he had no alternative to offer. All he knew was that the world had become too complex for him, that he had to make something of himself before too long, something that would break the ugly cycle. He needed to do something where he could have power over his chances, his own power, and not to be dependent upon the white man's beneficence.

He doesn't know when it first crossed his mind; perhaps it was always there. But sometime after they buried his father, he began to speak of it: he wanted to have a business of his own. He didn't know what kind of business. He had had no experience in any specific field. It was all so amorphous and farfetched; his friends said, sure, but they laughed at him. What? How? Where you gonna get the money? Man, you might as well hitchhike to Hollywood to become a movie star!

He persisted, knowing all the limitations. He understood their scepticism, rooted in the reality of all their lives. But his ambitiousness dominated his thinking and his actions, for he needed to live in a certain way.

He went back to work, took the same rotten jobs with the same lousy pay. But this time he saved his money, as much as he could. He worked evenings, too, sometimes at his brother John's after-hours place, conveniently located directly under their apartment. It was a place for neighborhood people to hang out, have a few drinks, nothing disruptive but nonetheless illegal. "Another hustle" as Larry would put it. "The black man in the ghetto seems to spend his life going from one hustle to another, and they never last too long. On this one, one night coming near Christmas, two holdup men came in there, whipped out their pistols, made everyone strip naked and toss their clothes in the center of the floor. They were taking money out of the pockets when my momma came home, and she happened to glance through a hole in the floor. She saw what was going on and right away, she called the police. They came while everybody was still naked, and they grabbed the two thieves. It wasn't much of a victory, though: we didn't get our money back and the cops closed the place down. The way it all worked out, momma might as well have been working for the cops, not my brother."

He took other odd jobs. He washed cars. He ran errands. When he shot dice, it was no longer wild and undisciplined; he played to come out ahead, settling for a few dollars rather than risking a bundle. He was saving his money.

"The cops . . . they would smell out a game like they had radar. They'd come busting into the room so fast you could barely reach for your pile, much less rake it in. I mean, they came for that money themselves. 'We need the money for evidence,' they'd say. They'd pull us all into the wagon for violating the law against public gambling, and we'd be booked and jailed, but we never saw any of that 'evidence' presented to the judge or the sergeant or anyone, and we never got any of it back. Nobody ever asked about it, either. You ask one too many questions and you never know what else you might get booked for. I spent my third night in jail. I was getting to feel like it was a natural thing, like going to the dentist, or something . . ."

Then he met Jacqueline McBeth, the girl with the large soft eyes. She was bright and handsome and walked with her head high. She knew how to handle herself, knew what to say and when to say it. She was young, but she'd had plenty of experience in living. She was ambitious in the best sense, working her way through nursing school. He could not help himself, even if he'd wanted to. He fell in love with her.

"Love . . . man, I didn't know what it meant. How is it supposed to be? You'd get that fine feeling of wanting to be with someone, your heart beats like it's a bongo, you don't know what else you're doing, just making out with her till your head is going to come apart, it's that groovy. I mean, what happens next?

"I was doing fine with Jacqueline. She was a fine girl. I stopped all my crummy hustles and went back to the New York State Employment Agency trying to get a decent job, but like always, they had none. So I bought me a job. Hudson Vitamin Company, where the private agency takes $15 a week out of your salary. I was back in the clean-shirt rat race again. I was in love.

"I dreamed of a life with her. She'd be a nurse, making good money. I'd have a business. I didn't know what, but it'd be something. We'd have a decent apartment, we'd fix it up nice, all our own, and we'd live there with her two kids she'd gotten out of wedlock.

"She liked the dream, and after about eight months being together, we got married. Wow, I finally got married. I was twenty-five years old and I was gonna do okay. I had that feeling, you know; everything was going to be fine.

"Loving someone is one thing, living together is another, and being married is a third. Like I asked, what happens next? I was trying hard to fix up my life, but it wasn't working with her. I was having troubles with my job, the usual. I just couldn't accept it too well. I mean, I would sit there on the bench with maybe forty or fifty others, and I'd watch the vitamins go by on the belt, one after another, watching to see that the right colors are in the right bottles, day after day, always the same thing. I was working under another screwy foreman and I guess I'd be a little edgy when I got home. I needed sympathy, I needed the warm loving hand. But somehow, we got into arguments. Man, we had some big ones, mostly about money. We'd argue too much and too hard. Like I used to think it was necessary to have a marriage budget about money. Before payday, we had to decide what money we were going to spend, how and on what. But she would go out and spend her money on anything she fancied. She was individual about money; I wanted to be together.

"She had those two kids when I married her. No father. One

was aged three, a boy, the other five, a girl. I liked them. I tried to be a father to them. They were very nice and we got along fine. I'd read to them, tell them stories, teach them things like how to draw. I'd draw them pictures. They liked all that. They liked me, too. I would spend more time with the kids than she did, and that bothered me.

"Especially when she said she wanted to have another baby with me. I didn't. I just didn't think it was right. We didn't have the stability. I don't really know why, but she would cry about that. It became a big thing with her. Even bigger than the arguments about the money. I guess she thought she could seal up the marriage by having a kid with me.

"One morning at breakfast, I was feeling awful. I could see she was stewing over something and I asked her, don't stew over me. Not today. I didn't want any trouble, my head was feeling like it was squeezed in a vice. But she couldn't hold it in. I guess her head wasn't feeling too good either. She came at me like she wanted to drill me into the floor and I just exploded. I slapped her. Blam! First time in my life I hit a woman. She looked at me like I'd thrown a knife at her or something, and then suddenly she became very calm, very thoughtful. I thought, wow, this slapping thing isn't bad. I mean, I'd heard of guys who did it all the time, but I could never go with that before. But there she was, quiet as a mouse, and then all she said was that she was going out to get some bacon and eggs because we were out of them. Well, she was gone a long time, and I drank some coffee, listened to the radio, wondering what was holding her up, when there was a knock on the door. There she was, sure enough, and instead of those bacon and eggs, she'd brought two police with her!

"Wow, I didn't need that.

" 'Did you strike this woman?' they asked me.

" 'This is my wife,' I said.

" 'Is this man your husband?' they asked her.

" 'Yes, but I want him out of here,' she said.

" 'This is my house,' I said. 'You can't throw me out of my own house.'

" 'He's right,' they told her. 'If you want to press charges and go to court, well, do it that way . . .'

"I thought that was the first time I ever had a cop on my side.

"I tried to straighten it out with her, but she wasn't buying nothing from me. After a while, I guess I saw the truth clear enough. The whole thing with her was just another failure. I didn't know why it should have to end, but we weren't going to stay together just to keep on doing all that arguing and suffering. I knew it was over.

"I left. I walked over to Lexington Avenue a couple of blocks away and got me a room. I had to borrow $15 from a friend to pay for it. It was a grubby room, and nothing in it was mine. It was a lonely hole and that's what it would always be. It was the opposite of my dream of a married life, the very opposite, but there I was, as real as could be, and it didn't matter one bit that I didn't really know what had gone wrong this time.

"Still, I was not all the way down. I had something going for me: Jacqueline's mother—her name was Gladys Brockington—a very fine woman, especially for a mother-in-law, had found me this store on the corner of Lafayette and Stuyvesant. She knew how much I wanted a business of my own, and she found this vacant spot. She told me it would be up to me to make something out of it. I thought, wow, all I needed was the money to begin, to fix it up, get the equipment, stock it with merchandise, that's all. Well, I asked her if she wanted to go into business with me, but she said no. All she wanted was to go fifty-fifty on the rent which I could repay her out of profits, a very generous offer.

"The trouble was, I was broke again. I took another job, this time driving a private cab. I moved to the house of a lady I'd known for a long time and met her brother-in-law, James Blakely. He had some money, so we started talking about business, and he decided he would like to join me in getting it going.

He had the capital and I had the ambition. Blakely was an engineer up at N.Y.U. and he didn't have much experience in business either. We'd talk for hours about what kind of a place it ought to be.

"Finally we agreed. It ought to be a food store. After all, like they say: 'People gotta eat!' "

6

"Well, it was something, opening that store. There was no brass band, no big searchlights, no ribbons and pennants, no TV stars, no nothing. I just opened the store that day, August 25, 1966. There was a sign on the window, L&S FOOD STORE, and there was a sign on the wall inside, LAURENCE BLUTCHER, PROP. It was mine —in part, anyway—and it was like I was a woman and had just given birth to a beautiful baby. I was twenty-nine years old and I was thinking, I finally found a way to make some sense out of my life. My mother, she came over and bought a sack of groceries, and my sisters came, and people in the neighborhood started coming in, and others I knew, and I was proud that I could show them that I was doing this for myself."

It had been a difficult month of preparation. His partner, James Blakely, had put up $1100, and Larry had scraped together $250 more, borrowing from his sister and others, a little here, a little there. He had to use up almost all his cash for equipment: food freezer and refrigeration were the most vital and most expensive, and he had almost nothing left to stock them. This is what hurt him most: there was no credit offered on merchandise.

"It wasn't an easy business, that much I could see right from the beginning. I had to put in all kinds of hours. My partner had his own job at N.Y.U. and he was hardly ever there. It was just me. I didn't know much about the grocery business, but it started out okay, right from the beginning. I guess that made the later part tougher to take. We'd started out with vegetables and canned goods, and a few staples like bread and milk, and then we got more equipment for meats and fish, even. The stuff was moving, all right. I kept my own records, bookkeeping, and everything was just the way it was supposed to be. Sometimes, I would work until two in the morning to get it all down in the books. But I learned. I had to. There wasn't anyone else.

"My partner saw I was turning out a good trade, and after six or eight months, he wanted to buy me out. But I wouldn't sell. In fact, he said to me, 'Look, either you let me buy you out or give me enough money to buy my part.' I went to my family, hoping we could somehow swing it together. My brother Bill was home on leave from the Air Force, and he came to see the store in operation. He loaned me $650 to pay my partner, and the rest I would have to pay off out of profits. Blakely, he said okay, he would give me eight months to pay off. That was in March 1967. I would have to make payment in November."

Air Force Technical Sergeant Bill Blutcher was proud of his brother. On this visit to New York, he spent more time with Larry than usual. "I'd noticed the change in Larry over the last few years. I hadn't seen him very much because of where I'd been stationed, but I thought he used to be, well, irresponsible. He'd gamble dice and shoot away money without seeming to care whether he won or lost. A man without worries. Me, I could never understand a man who didn't worry. He thought mostly about himself and never seemed to care about anything else, not having a family or anything to root him down. But when he got the store, that was something different. It was something he really wanted. I could see that. Anyone could see that. He was determined; he was going to make his living in that store. He worked hard. I felt downright proud of him, for the first time, I guess. He was trying to carry his own weight . . ."

Larry had discovered the essence of the businessman's ethic: ownership as the spur to profit-seeking. No man could possibly have been more deeply committed.

"Wow, I was putting in twelve-fourteen hours a day. Seven days a week. I needed help and I needed stock, but it takes money for that. I thought, if I could get a beer license, I could double my business. People would come in to buy beer, and then they would buy other things. If you don't have beer, they don't come in. Beer was the thing. There was a food store directly across the street run by a Puerto Rican named Marrero Ponce, and I could see how much more business he was doing just because he had beer. The way I saw it, there was enough business for both of us, but he didn't like the competition. He tried to stop the delivery men from coming to my store. The bread man and Drake's Cake man. The Pepsi man. A few others. The delivery men told me about this. They said Ponce threatened to cut their orders if they delivered to me, too. But they came anyway.

"But it was beer that I needed. I got my sister's lawyer, Frederick Douglass, to help me file an application for a license. On it, you have to put down your police record, but I was warned by a friend that if you have too many arrests, they don't give you a license. That shook me up some, because when I started to list them, there were four. The attempted assault charge; the policy fine; the two crap-shooting arrests. I guess I ran scared at the size of that list. It read like I was some kind of a ferocious criminal. I pictured all those white political hacks looking at it and shaking their heads: 'No, sir, that black boy isn't fit to handle beer.' So I left one of the arrests off, the attempted assault. It was dumb, all right. I suppose I thought if I didn't say anything about it, nobody would know.

"They knew. They found out easily enough, just checking the police files, and they turned me down:

The Authority finds that, in view of the false material statement made by the applicant together with his overall conduct of law observance, it would create a high degree of risk in the administration and control of the Alcoholic Beverage Commission Law to approve this application. Therefore, the Authority determines that public advantage and convenience would not be served to approve this application.

"Well, they got me both ways. Mr. Douglass tried to appeal it, but it was no use. I was not only a criminal, I was also a liar.

"I just kept struggling with the store, without beer. I was living on Palmetto Street, about a mile away, so I'd fix myself meals on a hot plate I had in the store. Sometimes I'd eat three meals a day there. I'd walk back and forth to my place, but when the weather was too rough and I'd be too tired, I would take a taxi, it was the only other way. I had to cut that out, though; I figured I'd have to sell a whole case of canned goods just to pay for a single cab fare in order to sell the canned goods. I mean, that didn't make sense. Still, there were times when I'd just be too tired . . .

"One thing, I was learning the grocery business. The hard way, all right. I learned that what looked like a lot of business, when the bookkeeper tallied it up, it was not so much at all. In my first business profit-and-loss statement, covering from August 25, when I opened, to the end of the year 1966, I took in a total of $5,028.59 worth of business. My purchases of stock came to $3,455.68, and my operating expenses were $712.74. My net profit, then, was only $860.17. The way I figured it, with the time I put in, I was working for less than sixty cents an hour!

"What I needed was a faster-moving stock. I needed full

shelves and a big assortment of groceries. If I couldn't have beer, I needed other things all the more. I needed stock, and in order to get it, I needed credit. But when they found out that most of my business was done on credit, again I was dead. It just didn't work both ways. I couldn't help that. It was a neighborhood mostly on welfare and small weekly paychecks. People didn't have much cash. If they do, they go to the supermarkets where the shelves are full and there are bargains. The L&S Food Store had to function on paper. I'd take in a hundred dollars on a fair day, maybe, and my cash register wouldn't have $30 in it. Just a lot of names on a pad.

"So I tried to get a loan. I applied to the Brooklyn Small Business Development Opportunities Corporation, and began to fill out forms. I got a few respectable people [white] to write those To Whom It May Concern letters for character references. I had my bookkeeper list all my assets, the turnover, the equipment I had, and tried to get them to lend me a thousand dollars. It took several weeks, and then they turned me down.

"I couldn't get credit and I couldn't get a beer license and I couldn't get a loan.

"And then the cops started coming around. It was about that time, early in 1967, they'd be buzzing around the block, especially on Sundays, and then they would stop, come in, and look around like they were casing the place. Then one Sunday they wrote out a summons: Violation of the Sabbath Law. I had to go down to Police Court and pay a five-dollar fine. But I also had to stay open on Sundays. The way I figured it, I took in more than twice as much on Sundays as I did on any other day.

"Then, the police came around again. One of them, Officer Repaci, I recognized him from a visit before, he said to me: 'Look here, you can't be open on Sunday. You have to close up or you know what you have to do . . .' It's funny, no one had ever asked me for a bribe before; the first time you hear it, though, you know right away what they mean. You hear about it so much, all over the neighborhood, it gets so you expect it every time you see a policeman. So I reached into the cash register and kicked over to the two of them, two dollars each.

"I stewed about that some. Hell, I couldn't get four dollars' credit for a couple of cases of biscuits even . . .

"The trouble was, business never seemed to get any better. Not for any length of time. There'd be a flurry of action one day, maybe even for a few days, and then it would die off. I'd stay open later and later, hoping maybe I could develop a midnight trade. That, too, would die out. And all the time, I was having trouble with the credit people.

"Like there was one lady, Mrs. Smart was her name. She had eleven kids and she was on welfare. She'd come in and clean me out of stock. She'd take the cans off the shelf, four here, six there, eight more here, and there'd be hardly anything left, and then she'd insist on credit. She would take the last of my stock and I wouldn't have a quarter to show for it. Then I'd have to try and collect. It was a regular war. She'd take weeks to pay, always keeping ahead of me, paying back a little here, a little there, then taking more of my stock. She was always angry when I went around to collect. The trouble was, you had to keep giving her credit because if you stopped, she would take off for another store and leave you stuck with the credit you'd given her. She wouldn't pay. It ended up, she took me for $20. It sure was a permanently nervous situation.

"It was wild, all the different kinds of people who came in. Mostly, there was no trouble. I was never robbed or anything. I was never afraid of it. Not while I was open. There just wasn't that much money or stock to be robbed. Besides, I knew most everyone in the neighborhood. There were drunks every once in a while, though, and they'd come in and fall all over the place, and you'd have to let them sleep it off. There was one drunk, a white man, came in late one Saturday night with his young white wife. She wanted a pack of cigarettes. He was having a fight with her, and he was mad. He was going to beat her up, right there in my store, and I had to grab him to stop him. I got him into a taxi finally but it was really something. I thought that was the end of it, but then, an hour later, there she was, the wife, all by herself. I mean, wow, it was real late and all, and I knew she didn't come all the way back for more cigarettes. She started talking and I started sweating. I didn't go for the black-man–white-woman scene. I guess I have a built-in resistance to that. Like my brother Bill says, what it gets down to, no white man is ready to accept the black man as an equal rival for a white woman. It's ingrained in the American mind. The white man, he doesn't want to see the black man with his girl—and especially not his wife. To him, it's like the pig and the chicken discussing ham and eggs. The chicken, he says he likes it, but the pig, he don't. He says to the chicken: 'You're just making a contribution. But me, I'm making a sacrifice.'

"I sure worked hard to get that lady into a taxi."

Larry's life became somewhat easier when he moved into an apartment at 960 Lafayette, directly over the store. It was an old building, maybe sixty years old, with just a few apartments and store fronts. The owner, Dominic LaScala, had bought it for $6000 but, as Larry speculated, "I think he was sorry he did. The staircase was falling apart and you never knew when it would crumble and what would go with it. Still, I had four rooms. All to myself. It was a perfect set-up if I had a woman. I really needed a woman, someone to work with me, to help me with the store, to share it all with me. The trouble was, every woman I came across, all they wanted was credit in the store. They wanted to take away from me, not help me. I wanted to use them, I guess, and they sure as heck wanted to use me. Wow, it was pitiful.

"Then, one day last summer, out of the living blue, my wife, Jacqueline, popped in on me. I hadn't seen her in a year or so. I looked into those beautiful big round eyes and I could feel something flaking inside me. I knew it was bad news, like I was made of jelly, all soft and mushy. I was letting those eyes drag me where I didn't want to go. Right away, I could see why I had fallen for her. It was all there in the first look at her again. Oh, I knew that there was trouble waiting behind her. I surely did know that. But I guess I must've been really lonely, because I wanted her back.

"I said it to her, let's get back together again. She was making good money as a private nurse. Like $34 a day, or so she told me. She had a car, too. With a car, that would be perfect for me. I could go get stock while she clerked the store. We could build together, we could make the store work.

"She listened to me, listening patiently. And when I finished, all she could say was that I was in the wrong type of business. Too much competition, all nickels and dimes. Maybe I should try a jewelry business, or at least a clothing store, she said. I argued with her. No, we could make it work. It didn't matter much about the bigger store across the street. Competition was good, it makes you work harder, do better. There are always going to be things working against you. The thing to do was to beat them.

"But I could see, we weren't going to get together. There just wasn't enough between us, at least not enough to want her to come in with me in this operation. And that was my pitch to her. She had to want that, too.

"I don't know why she popped in. She said, just because she wanted to say hello. But I knew it was more than that. I guess she must've been casing the set-up to see if she liked it. Or maybe she just wanted to see me again, to see how it felt to be with me. Women are like that, when they have nothing better to do, they have to play games with love. They come around with the big eyes and the soft smile and they say, here I am, let's see who wins this little game. Only thing, they know when to come around, like when the odds are all theirs. That's one game you can't beat them at, because you're always playing it by their rules.

"So she popped out just as quickly as she popped in. She left me behind that counter and in my four-room apartment upstairs, and I was stuck with that empty feeling again, only worse.

"I was sad, all right. Something like that happens, it reminds you how bad things are going. The store was in trouble and I'd been pretending too much, pretending that something was going to happen to turn the tide. I'd been pretending that all of a sudden business was going to pick up, or that I'd get a big juicy loan and put a lot of stock on my shelves, and everybody would come in and pick it clean, and I'd be on my way. But when Jacqueline walked out, I couldn't believe that any more. She hurt me in the heart, and now my head was aching, too.

"But I kept working, putting in the long hours, trying to make it go. One friend came through for me and loaned me a hundred dollars. Just to put stock on my shelves. It wasn't nearly enough, but it was something. I had something more to sell and when people came in, they could buy something more than a can of soup or some Drake's cakes.

"The cops, they came cruising around on Sundays with their hands out. Pretty soon it was three dollars here, three dollars there. I decided that I would close on Mondays. The way I'd heard it, it was okay to stay open Sundays if you closed on another day of the week. The cops said that themselves. 'We checked it; you're open seven days a week.' In the fall, I started closing on Mondays, took the day off. I wouldn't open the store. I wouldn't even go in it. I'd walk by it like it wasn't even mine. I'd lay around the apartment, or visit my brother, or hang around with friends, but I'd stay away from the store. Only thing was, I couldn't stop worrying about it.

"I worried about that store the way a mother worries about a sick baby. The doctor comes and examines it and shakes his head and you know there's bad trouble. But it's your baby, so you keep hoping it will get well and everything'll turn out fine. One afternoon, I'm sweeping up when this man comes in. A white man, and he talks a little like a foreigner. I'd never seen him before. He asked me if I wanted to buy a new cash register and a fine new slicing machine. I had to laugh at that. What the hell would I need *that* for! Man, I said, that's like trying to sell a pair of shoes to a man without feet.

"But he don't stop, this man. He starts telling me how beautiful this new cash register is. All electric, automatic, tallying up all the figures at every sale, punching out little slips with the name of my store on it, even has a secret compartment where you hide your big bills—everything high class and all. He looked at my old cash register and he said it only doubled my work, that it was completely out of style, but he'd give me a good trade-in on it. Same thing with my meat slicer. He'd sell me a new super slicer, also automatic, cuts slim and clean as a whistle. And then when I'm laughing and telling him I can't use it, he sees my problem. 'Look,' he says, 'if you buy these items, I'll see to it that you get stock on your shelves. I'll fix it up with certain people I know in your business who can get you credit. You're not getting any credit now, are you? Well, I can fix it up. When you buy this register, I'll get everything straightened out for you. You can pay for it when you sell your stock, month by month. Everything is going to change for you. I'll even fix it up so that you have a new grand opening, you know? We'll have pennants flying outside, balloons, give-away items. Everybody will come and you'll make a lot of money!'

"Well, I knew it was just a lot of crap. He was feeding me anything, trying to sucker me into buying. Hell, I didn't even trust that accent of his, it sounded so phony. But the more he rapped, the more I sort of leaned with it. I was so sick, I was ready to take anything for medicine. Crazy as it sounded, I couldn't help but think, well, maybe it was on the square. Maybe it would all work out. And then, I guess I didn't much care any more, like shooting your last ten bucks on rolling a four when the dice are as cold as a landlord's heart.

"The man, he sees me wavering. He says, 'Look, on Monday morning, I'm going to have this guy come and put a lot of Grand Opening stuff outside your store. And before that, he's going to arrange to have a full stock on your shelves. I'll see to that personally, the minute I leave here. All you have to do is sign this paper . . .'

"I felt like the biggest fool in the neighborhood, like the man who's supposed to have bought the Brooklyn Bridge, but this guy was a helluva rapper, all right. I signed. I bought the cash register and the slicer, and it came to a total of $670—$30 a month for two years. I put my name on the paper and no sooner did I do that when he shot out of there like my place was on fire.

"The next day, they brought me the new machines and took my old ones, but I kept waiting for Monday when the real action was scheduled to begin. Monday came around all right, but nobody came with it. No stock, no pennants, no Grand Opening. Nothing. I was even supposed to be closed on Mondays, but I opened. It was the same on Tuesday: nothing. On Wednesday, I called up the number of the company written on the contract: Equipment Equities Company, and asked for Mr. Sailor, the man who sold me the machines. There was a pause, and then a man gets on the phone and he asks what he can do for me. Well, I explained that I was told that I was going to get credit, that stock was going to be put on my shelves, that there was to be a Grand Opening and all, and that I wasn't going to be able to pay for the machines unless this was so. He said he didn't know about any of that, nobody had said anything to him about credit or stock or Grand Openings. I could see I wasn't going to get nowhere with him, so I told them to come pick up their machines and give me mine back and we'd forget the whole deal. Oh no, he said, I'd signed a contract and I had to go through with it, that was the way they did business. Suddenly, as he was talking, I realized that the man on the phone was the same guy who sold me, only he had switched from that fake foreign accent to his American voice. Suddenly he's telling me that the other voice who sold me the register had no right to make those promises and that I should not have accepted them, so I'd *have* to pay the $30 a month. I said, now wait, let me talk to Mr. Sailor, you know, like I was going along with him, and maybe him and me could straighten this thing out. And finally he says, 'Well you can't speak to him: we fired him!'

"I hung up the phone and I had to laugh. I laughed, but I felt real stupid. Wow, I'd sure asked for it. I'd just let them sucker me like I was born yesterday. It was like when I was a kid around ten, I remember how a bunch of white kids came by in the streets, and you could hear the music playing on their little radios, beautiful music, clear as a bell, right out there in the street. They stood around watching us toss bottle tops against the curb, surrounding us with all that music. They were friendly enough, and one of them showed me his radio. I never played a battery radio before but I let on like it was nothing. Then he said something like: 'There's more where this came from,' you know, getting us all worked up. He told us that there was this real old cruddy building with a lot of big boxes in there and he knew a way to get in, as easy as falling off a log, and that there had to be a hundred more of these radios, just asking to be taken, that nobody wanted them, you could tell. Well, we let those white kids show us. They said only two of us could come, me and another. They took us down about a mile to this place, an old warehouse type building, very small and beat up. You wouldn't think they'd keep anything in there, much less all those radios. Then the white boys led us around the back and pointed to a door, and you could see that the padlock was busted. They said they'd stand guard, and all we had to do was to be quick about it, and be sure not to test those radios in there lest some-one should hear. My buddy and me, we sneaked up to that door like we were soldiers attacking a German machine-gun nest, and then we pushed in as fast as we could. It was dark in there, and smelled of dampness and moldy dirt, and for a minute or two, we couldn't see a thing. Then we heard them, a million rats, squeaking and scurrying all over the place, and when we could see, that was all there was, just the rats, and not a radio or a box in the whole place. And as quick as we saw this, the white boys were just as quick in slamming the door behind us, jamming a stick or something into the hasp that locked the door, and we were trapped with all those rats. Wow, it was horrible. It took us maybe twenty minutes to get out of there, we had to smash a window and climb through the broken glass with all those rats squiggling at our feet. And when we got out, there they were, playing their radios again, standing there laughing at us.

"So now I walked over to that new cash register thinking how I hadn't thought of that rat scene for a long time. Sucker then, sucker now. I was still looking for the beautiful music, still thinking that the white man was going to lead me to it. I stared at that cash register feeling like the big damn fool I was. I punched the No Sale button and the drawer sprung open with that fancy ring, like the gong at a prize fight. I flipped the lever that lets you get to the secret place 'to hide your big bills,' only there were no big bills in it. There was nothing in it, not even a love letter. I put something in it all right: I spit in it.

"The police came the next Tuesday. They walked in, saying nothing at first, just looking around like maybe I was hiding something. A dozen beautiful blonde white slaves, maybe. They bought a pack of cigarettes, then they said: 'You were closed yesterday?' like they didn't really know, just reminding me they were keeping in touch. I said, 'Yes, you can ask Harry the Cop,' a black policeman who walked the beat across the street, on the 81st Precinct. So they nodded and left, and I got the message, all right.

But the next Monday, end of November it was, I had to stay open. On that day, it was a big payday, welfare checks and all, and there were all those people who owed me money. Credit people. I had to stay open to collect. The cops drove by, I saw them, Repaci and another, but I didn't care. I took in a lot of money that was owed me, and I even put $80 in the secret compartment. I knew they'd be coming around again on Sunday, but I'd face that when the time came."

That Sunday was December 3, 1967.

7

When police officers McCole and Repaci escorted the bleeding, handcuffed, stumbling figure of Larry Blutcher into the emergency ward of Cumberland Hospital, it was strictly a routine sight. There were no sickening gasps of horror, no indignant comments, barely a turning of heads. They walked him inside until an interne could get to him, and he lay there on the stretcher dizzy, only partially aware of pain and blood and consciousness. His hands were numb from the binding handcuffs. McCole stood over him for a while, in case he should lose consciousness again and topple off, while Repaci sought treatment for his injured thumb. Finally, they got to Larry.

"They wheeled me in and the doc went to work on me. They cleaned me up and discovered twelve different lacerations on my head. It took them sixty stitches to sew them together again. It took them a long time and I was getting awfully weak. I was hurting so much, I was still scared I wasn't going to make it. I'd never been so scared before . . . ."

Larry's older sister, Earvina, heard the news around 2 o'clock: "I was supposed to take my daughter to church that morning, but my brother Bill was in town on a weekend pass from Fort Meade and we sat around talking. He was just leaving to go back home when Bubba called from John's place, telling us how the police were coming to his store to make him pay off for being open on Sunday. I had advised him before to stay closed on Monday so he could legally stay open on Sunday since that was his best day for business. He had done this, so the police had no right to bother him. No right at all.

"It wasn't until later, in the afternoon, that John called and told me the news. Bubba had been beaten up! I hadn't hung up on John long when the phone rang again. It was a lady friend of mine, telling me the same, but worse. She said there was blood all over Lafayette Avenue in front of his store, that she had seen them drag him off in the car like he had to be dead.

"My heart stopped. It couldn't be!

"Right away, I called the 79th Precinct and they told me Bubba had been taken to Cumberland Hospital where he was being treated in the emergency ward. I called my mother, in case she hadn't heard, and then I called my lawyer, Mr. Frederick Douglass. (Luckily, he was in his office, even though it was Sunday. He'd been my lawyer for years and we worked together in investments and real estate deals. I'd met him through my work in the Democratic and also the Republican parties when I was sixteen. I used to help out there, for fun, very social, stamping letters, getting people to come out and vote and all. It didn't matter much about the politics of it. I never cared who won.)"

Vina is the type of women one wants on his side, especially during an emergency. She had always been blessed with a remarkable capacity for knowing what to do, with the energy and resourcefulness to do it. "Leave it to Vina," the family would say whenever there was a crisis. She seemed to thrive on them. She had trained as a nurse but was forced out of the profession when a 250-pound patient rolled off a hospital bed: when Vina tried to restrain her, she severely strained her back. She was herself hospitalized as a result and eventually declared 75 per cent disabled. She was determined to be active, however; she studied real estate and became a licensed realtor, buying and selling properties in Brooklyn. It was typical of her that for all her persistent back pains, she avoided narcotic pills to relieve them, having seen too much addiction that resulted from this sort of problem. She preferred to wear back braces for support, disciplining herself against the constant discomfort. It was a rare event when anyone heard Vina complain.

She lived at St. John's Place, outside Bedford-Stuyvesant in an area of Brooklyn bordered by Crown Heights and Ocean Hill-Brownsville. "When I moved here a dozen years ago, it was almost all Jewish. Now it's all black."

She was on her way out when her younger sister—Lilian, Larry's twin—came over, and together they taxied to the hospital. "It was around 2:30 or so. Mr. Douglass got there a few minutes later, and then my mother. There were a lot of others milling around. They had come over from in front of the Precinct, right after the ambulance, I guessed. We asked to see Bubba, but they wouldn't let us. All I saw in the emergency ward was the policeman, Repaci, getting treatment on his left thumb. The other one, McCole, was standing with him, laughing at the bandage they were putting on.

"Finally, we heard that Bubba was in X ray. I knew my way around hospitals, so momma, Mr. Douglass, and I went to the X-ray room. We could see him through the window of the hall door. It was horrible what they were doing to him. I mean, he was in a comatose state, but the X-ray technicians stood him up to walk and he fell flat on the floor! The way I heard it, they had him on the critical list most of the afternoon. Why, he was unconscious until some time after 6:30!"

Lilian, nicknamed Tiny, was married to a carpenter, Al Stewart, and lived on Schenectady Avenue in a four-room apartment with two young children. By monetary standards, Tiny had done well. Al made good money, their neighborhood was better than most, they owned some real estate in the area and drove a good car. "The first I heard of it, momma called and sounded hysterical, said something that Bubba had been shot by the police. Right off, I called Vina and she said no, he'd been beaten up, that I should come right over, we would all go to the hospital. When we got there, though, they wouldn't let us see him. It was an accident that we did. They were wheeling him out the X-ray room on a stretcher, we could see him through the hallway door. Momma and I, we ran to him. He was all beaten up, his head as big as a lamp shade. It was like he was dead, he looked so horrible. I was sure he was going to die. I thought, even if he lives through this, he won't ever be any good any more . . ."

Mrs. Epsie Blutcher was preparing Sunday dinner for herself and her friend, James Smith, who had been close to her since the death of her husband in 1962, when Vina's call routed her from the kitchen. She was a sturdy woman who had lived through a fair share of troubled times, but this was news that genuinely frightened her. Why should the police do anything to Bubba? The fact that they did, the fact that they could do anything they wanted to, the fact that everything conceivable happened in Bedford-Stuyvesant, that was what frightened her. It was as if she had known all along. She had lived these last twenty-five years in a constant state of suspended fear, knowing that sooner or later something terrible was going to happen.

Still, she kept control of herself now, a quick, competent set of adjustments that took herself and Smith downstairs to a taxi and headed them for the hospital. It was a long ride, the streets were crowded, and time worked insidiously on her equanimity. She could not resist her thoughts any more and, like the popular image of the dying man seeing his whole life pass quickly before him, she reviewed the totality of her knowledge of her son. She was, as Larry had so often put it, a true Christian woman. Strictly reared on a faith in God and a dependence on her church, she had watched Larry go through his developing religious disaffection which she has resisted as a true believer must. She had disliked his troubled ways, his resulting failures, his unsuccessful love affairs and disastrous marriage. She had viewed his several unfortunate confrontations with the law as God's judgment upon his erring course. But when he finally opened his store, she had reveled in his rising sense of responsibility. She had always been proud of her children, all of them, appreciating their problems to the full extent of her understanding. She had felt for their struggle for a decent life, prouder still in the measure of success they had achieved, each in his own way. Indeed, compared with so many of her counterparts, she had raised them extremely well. She could stand before her Maker and justify her motherhood in His eyes.

Yet, through all the years of her unrelenting concern, she had feared. Her faith was always at war with her fear. She had dared to pluck her family from the familiar cocoon of countless generations in Georgia to challenge life itself in Brooklyn, to take the risk in order to gain a better chance for her children, to drop them into the strange and terrifying big city turmoil that they might climb out of the endless misery of Deep South peonage. This had been her doing, hers alone, and she could not but fear the consequences, especially, in recent years, as this applied to Larry.

She said nothing of this in the taxi. She sat there with Smith, staring out the window, silently urging the traffic to dissolve in front of them, repeating her daughter's message to herself over and over, telling herself that Vina had probably allowed herself too much emotion, that nothing so horrible had happened to her son, that, after all, Vina had only heard this and had seen none of it, and neither had John who had told her, that such reports are always exaggerated. Conveniently, she remembered earlier confrontations with this sort of thing, like the time her son Bill had been stabbed during an incident in a store. Someone had called her that he'd been taken away in an ambulance and, not knowing details, she had pictured him bleeding to death, only to rejoice in the reality which was infinitely less terrifying. Every mother knows this fear, she told herself. "It's probably nothing . . ." she said out loud. James Smith took her hand in his and nodded. It was as if he'd been thinking the very same thing.

However, the minute she saw the hospital her sense of impending disaster began building into hysterics. All the delays and milling about and blank stares only made matters worse. It seemed impossible to get to him, as though they were hiding him, deliberately, deceitfully. And when she finally saw him, was only an accident, and the circumstances were as grotesque as in a ghoulish Hollywood movie. "I saw him through the hall door. I don't know why but I knew it was Bubba. His head was in a big bandage and they were rolling him out of a room on a stretcher. And suddenly they turned, and Bubba started to fall off! I screamed. He was falling off the stretcher and they didn't care! He was drugged and unconscious and he was going to fall. The attendant just did manage to get a hand on him, and stopped his head from hitting the floor. It was the most terrible thing I'd ever seen."

When the Blutcher family left the hospital later that afternoon, they gathered in Vina's apartment to discuss what actions might be taken. Vina immediately attacked the telephone with the intensity of a fighter at his punching bag. She called the Police Commissioner, the Mayor's office, the Civilian Complaint Review Board, the Governor of New York State. She called the newspapers, radio stations, CORE, Brooklyn's own Sonny Carson, a militant former head of Brooklyn CORE. She even tried to get through to the President of the United States. She told them all what the police had done to her brother, and she let them know that the Blutcher family was not going to stand idly by and let that sort of brutality exist without kicking up a big fuss.

"Oh, they listened to me all right. They listened real good. They were all very polite and sympathetic, like it had just hap-

pened to one of their own. They all said they would send someone down to the hospital to investigate. They would do everything they could. And when I got off the phone, I sat down and
wrote a follow-up letter to the Civilian Complaint Review
Board; they should review this case at once. They should ask
McCole and Repaci, why the beating? What did Larry do to justify it? He was working on his own premises. There was no police call of trouble on those premises. Nothing had happened to
cause any kind of trouble. So why? What were those two police
doing there in the first place?"

Having seen so many of her fears justified, Mrs. Epsie Blutcher
spent most of the late afternoon fighting back tears. What sick-
ened her most was the inexplicability of it. "He was trying so
hard, so honest, so determined. He hadn't done nothing wrong.
It just chills my spine to think of what human beings will do to
another of a different race. That's all it was, the black thing. It
would never have happened to a white man. My God, don't everybody know that!"

When Vina finished calling every political "V.I.P" she could
think of, she started calling all the family friends. She called Bill,
who had just gone back to Fort Meade, asking him to come right
back to Brooklyn. He said he would. She asked everyone to call
the hospital to find out how Larry was doing. "It was a way to
scare them. To kick up some action, to show them we cared. Oh,
they all did it, too. When we got back to the hospital around
8:30 that night, there were over a hundred calls already, actually
jamming the switchboard, and they kept on coming. I could see
the difference in their attitude, as soon as we came in. They were
a lot more respectful toward the Blutchers, let me tell you."

Cumberland Hospital is a city institution, its history dating
back to 1879. Typically, it has grown many times its original size,
adding new wings to old with the usual annexes to supplement
the ever-expanding demands on its overworked facilities. As a
city hospital in Brooklyn, it cares for a large percentage of colored patients, and the violence and inhumanity of the ghetto is

89

inherent in the sight and smell of its wards. And, like any city institution, it is sensitive to any formidable pressure put upon it by a group of irate citizens—especially when the police department shows its own fears over a patient in its custody.

The phone calls accomplished their purpose. If the admission of Laurence Blutcher had been a routine action, it was no longer treated as such. And when it was realized later that afternoon that he had not yet recovered consciousness from the drugs and the injury, not only the Blutchers were worried.

An atmosphere of considerable tension greeted their return around 8:30 that Sunday evening, and they waited in the hall on the fourth floor prison ward under the somewhat nervous supervision of the ever-present police. Around 9:10, they were told that the patient had regained consciousness, that he was no longer in any danger.

"He was almost unrecognizable," his twin sister, Tiny, said. "It just didn't look like Bubba. The whole thing was so horrible, the way he was handcuffed, with the police hovering over him, I couldn't believe this had happened to him."

Also attending was a representative of the Mayor, Captain Gerard Kernis from the New York City Police Commissioner's Office. In Vina's presence, then, he came in to interview the patient. The patient was barely communicative.

"It was all a blur. I opened my eyes and I didn't know where I was. Maybe it was the drugs, I don't know what they had given me, or maybe it was what the cops had done to my head. The room was swimming all around me and I heard voices that came out of the distance. It was like a dream and I didn't dare move. I thought maybe I was dead and I got scared. Then I could feel how much my head was hurting and I remembered. And when I saw Vina, finally, I knew I was okay.

"They propped me up some and gave me some water and I drank it through a straw. I looked at momma and Vina and Tiny and I saw how they were keeping back their tears. Especially momma. I felt so weak, I couldn't hardly move. Then Vina told me that there was this police captain there and he wanted to ask me some questions. Oh, he was very nice. He asked me how I felt and everything, and said he wanted to know exactly what had happened, that I should tell him in my own words. Did the policemen ask for money? Had I seen them before? I told him. I told him everything. I thought later, even supposing he believed me—they say you don't lie when you've got all those drugs in you—what was the police captain going to do? Heck, I'd been telling it all to the enemy."

Vina stayed with the action, making certain that everything was done for her brother that could be done. All avenues of investigation were pursued. Later she met with Lieutenant Holton, also from the Commissioner's office. She spoke with a reporter from the New York *Daily News* who said his paper would cover the story only when it went to trial. Newspaperman George Todd from the *Amsterdam News* was more co-operative. He filed his story that night. Vina also met with representatives from Brooklyn CORE who promised that further discussions would take place.

When Captain Kernis finished talking with Larry, Vina immediately asked that he implement their visitation privileges, especially for their mother. "He was so nice, I began to suspect him. He was so sympathetic, so helpful, it got to be hard to take. I mean, he even got to taking us back and forth from the hospital in his car. Was this going to be some kind of a snow job?"

Epsie Blutcher was thankful for her daughter, knowing she could not have accomplished any of this herself. She could barely cope with the whole notion of her boy lying there suffering.

"Yes, I saw my son again that night. He was cleaned up some and he was conscious. They had his head all bandaged and he could speak to me, but his voice sounded so weak, I had all I could do not to cry some more. What hurt me so was that they had the poor half-dead boy handcuffed to the bed. My God, where did they think he was going to run to?"

8

Sunday night, December 3, 1967, was a night of sustained anger for the Blutchers. They met at two gatherings, one at Vina's, the other at John's. They weren't planned meetings, they just happened. Indeed, if they had been planned, the Blutchers would have all come together and worked out a course of action. As it happened, however, there was mostly talk and commiseration. Troubled, confused, angry people repeating to each other the causes of their distress. At Vina's, they talked until very late, tossing all sorts of suggestions into the pot. Petitions to the police, to the Mayor's office. Letters of protest to the newspapers. More and more telephoning. It was a woman-dominated group.

At John's apartment on Lafayette Avenue, the discussion ran hotter than anticipated. There were mostly men there and they spoke of the need to do something more extreme, something to shake up the police, to let them know they couldn't keep beating on blacks. There was mention of a march down to the 79th Precinct, tying up traffic, a big protest demonstration in defiance of all regulations. Then there were others, far more rebellious, ready and willing to really set things on fire. It was only talk at this point, but John knew enough to sense the feel of danger. Sometimes when people start talking—and if they go on enough —they can talk themselves into doing something they'd be better off not doing. The trouble was, his own emotion was so great he repeatedly found himself in their camp.

In the end, there was agreement by telephone between the two parts of the family. It was decided that they would hire an attorney to handle the criminal case against Larry. What with all their concern about his injury, they had scarcely noted that he had been charged with assault and resisting arrest. Epsie's friend, James Smith, knew of a lawyer who would be excellent for the defense, a militant, black, civil rights, and political leader named Conrad Lynn. Smith called him at his home in Rockland County, and it was arranged that the family would meet with him in his office on Monday morning.

Vina, for one, got very little sleep. The tensions of the day wreaked havoc on her bad back, and she could make no move without anguish. Though she had had years of practical hospital experience, the memory of the way her brother looked and the nature of the treatment brought on a new round of anxiety. She dreamt sinister dreams of the police and medics in a macabre conspiracy to kill him. She shook them off as a nightmarish hallucination, in part the product of her own discomfort. But in the morning, as soon as she awoke, she called the hospital to be certain of his health. And then she called the Civilian Complaint Review Board again, this time requesting some manner of protection for Larry. A few minutes later, realizing she was dealing with "the enemy," she called the Mayor's office, remembering the warmth of their initial response, and there, too, she asked for extra protection.

"It was weird. A few minutes later, someone else from the Mayor's office called me because they'd heard that the people around the 79th Precinct were going to riot. They wanted me to stop them. And what was really weird was that the Police Commissioner's office called right after that and said the exact same thing!"

Whoever had circulated the threat of such action was not far off base. The events in front of the 79th Precinct and the jamming of the switchboard at Cumberland Hospital were certainly not typical, especially not in winter. According to tradition, cold weather was supposed to discourage mass protest. The tensions of Bedford-Stuyvesant, however, were sufficient to any season. One might speculate that *because* it was December, grievances had accumulated for several months without release, that the time was ripe for the normal pattern to be upset.

There was no doubt but that the brutal beating of Larry Blutcher was the talk of the neighborhood. The L&S Food Store at 960 Lafayette Avenue suddenly became a well-known attraction, and many gathered there on Monday, rehashing the gory details, somewhat resentful of Sunday's rain, for it had washed away all traces of blood in the streets. It was suggested, not without irony, that if Larry had had an active partner to open the store that Monday, with an adequate stock he might have grossed enough to pay for a private room in a first-rate hospital, so many of the neighbors had come. The police drove by, cautious in their uncertainty. A temporary phenomenon, everyone knew. The intensity of all wars has a way of shifting with the rise and fall of passions. Meanwhile, the talk in the streets was angry talk. They all knew the store and they all knew how Larry had struggled with it and they could not justify what the police had done to him. Indeed, there was hardly a storekeeper on Stuyvesant Avenue who did not claim to have faced the same sort of problem. Food stores, candy stores, barber shops, cleaning shops, liquor stores. It was all the same:

"Cops . . . they don't have no names. Just numbers and guns."

"They come 'round. Sure. They come 'round with that gimme look and they smile like it was just a joke, that's all. A smile for a two-dollar payoff and everybody's friends. Sure. But if you ain't got the two dollars ready, the smile is gone before you can blink."

"Yeah, I got trouble here sometimes. Sheeit, you can't breathe without there being trouble. Onct, two young studs come in . . . gonna help theirselves to beer and stuff. They so tough they ain't even gonna steal, you know what I mean? They just help theirselves, four-five dollars worth, then they walk away. Sure, I call the police, and twenty minutes later, here they come, and they ask a hunnerd questions and do nothing but take a beer for theirselves too. Sheeit, I got trouble, but I wouldn't call no more police."

"There ain't no way a man can duck 'em. It's like trying to stay dry in a rain storm. I bet a guy once he couldn't run three blocks down Lafayette Avenue without getting stopped by the fuzz. [Laughter] Sheeit, a nigger's gotta walk real slow or they think he's just robbed someone."

They all talked. They fed their anger with words and, eventually, expended their anger with words, for everyone knew that the blood in the street was the message the police had intended to leave. The police had to have their way, one way or another, and only a fool would defy it.

And though they did not say it, they thought of the blood and whose it was: it was Larry Blutcher who had been the fool.

John Blutcher was there, ostensibly to check on the store. Vina came by, and they talked about having a photographer take pictures of the wreckage on the floor that might prove valuable as evidence. Air Force Sergeant Bill Blutcher had dutifully returned from Fort Meade, Maryland, and he too was there. They all talked with neighbors in a mutual sharing of anger, but no one knew what anyone could do about it.

To Bill, it was the kind of turmoil that was jarringly alien to his life. He was thirty-six, a year or so younger than John. He had spent his entire maturity in the service, sixteen years, and had achieved for himself all the attitudes of a sensible, secure existence. He had left home at twenty, traveled all over the world with various changes of base, from his home state of Georgia to the excitement of England. There used to be a glamour and sophistication about Bill, especially to Larry and his twin sister, Tiny, the two youngest. He appeared to have found an answer to the life-struggle, and that added to his dignity in eyes of the family. This he abetted through extensive reading, expanding his vocabulary and his knowledge of the world—one who had something to say and knew how to say it. He was, in fact, the most learned and articulate of the Blutchers, cultivating a comfortable, poised, pipe-smoking style. Bill was the family's closest bid for middle-class status.

It was not surprising. Even as a boy, there always had been something special about him. When he was graduated from Metropolitan High School in New York City, he had done extremely well. He had been elected president of the G.O.—the General Organization, to which all students belong—president of his graduating class. As he put it: "I had academic potential, too. I seriously entertained the idea of going to college. I thought I'd go to night school to make up whatever subjects I was lacking . . ." However, after a brief experience working at a Harlem drugstore, though he found pharmaceutical work satisfying, he decided on a less challenging career in the Air Force. "One of my buddies got killed in the Infantry in the Korean War. I never heard of anyone I knew getting killed in the Air Force."

A man can spend his whole professional life in the Armed Forces and never see a man die. Bill Blutcher, who never professed to be an adventurer, was more horrified by what had happened to his brother than anything he saw in the service. He was stunned by the sight of Larry in the hospital—and, in the end, terribly confused. He did not want this sort of thing to happen, not only because it had been done to his brother, but because it upset his protected view of America.

"I couldn't hardly believe they would do this to him. Larry was never that kind of boy. I remember how he was from way back when we were kids. Sure, we were all sort of different, but he was never a troublemaker. I mean, even I had some brushes with street gangs. You couldn't help but have them. But I always tried to avoid them. It was too easy to get into a pattern if you did. Trouble has a way of repeating, like a habit.

"It was a good family. My parents were together. My father, he was easy to communicate with. He was a man who enjoyed his children. Maybe, in a way, he was even nicer to Larry because Larry was younger. Parents can sense their mistakes bringing up the older ones and so were nicer to the younger. Poppa would sit and tell jokes and stories to us . . . but he would also tear your bottom up if he thought you were going bad.

"No, I can't really understand this thing. Even though most of my contacts with the law have not been pleasant, I can maintain my objectivity. But when someone says something about police brutality, I would guess there was substance to it. The American attitude toward cops has always been the kind that thinks of cops as nice simple guys doing a job, the friendly Irishman helping kids across the street and all that. And there's a lot of truth to that, too. Oh, I've been humiliated by the law. I've been stopped and shook down now and then, you know, as a suspect. You get to expect that sort of thing. Happens all the time, wherever you are in this country. It's part of a black man's life. But mostly, I always sort of pitied the cop, the honest cop who comes on the force and wants to do his job. Only thing, after six months or so, he gets to know how the system works and he has to accept it no matter what he thinks about it. Bribes, shakedowns, they're everyday things in the ghetto. It's been going on for years.

"I guess things are changing now. I mean, about the people. People are becoming smarter, better educated. They want more out of life. They don't want to settle so easy for the same old nonsense. They're gonna talk back. They're gonna refuse. Like Larry. He didn't want to keep on taking their guff. People want to assert themselves, they're not willing to lay down no more. But the trouble is, the cops still think they can beat on the black man and get away with it. It's accepted by the white people. That's the way they think it's always been and always will be. It's like it's supposed to be that way.

"You take a black man in the ghetto, he wants to find a way to make a decent living without stealing. He doesn't want to have to get up at, say, five in the morning to steal the milk in front of a store before the owner gets there, just to make himself a few dollars to play around with. He wants a job he can do. A decent job. A cop is the same guy in a way, trying to make his way so he can carry his own weight and be a part of society. To pay taxes, that's the sign. To get so you pay some income tax and carry your own weight.

"I'm different from Larry because I've been in the Air Force. I've always had three hots and a cot. I've never had to fight it out in the ghetto. I've had security. That's what the service gives you. A home. But if this thing had happened to me, I guess I would have really been mad. I would have flipped, man. You would have seen me with a stepladder and a little U.S. flag and I would've been sounding off my anger. I would have become an agitator. Definitely. It's weird, though: I can see why the cops do what they do. Like I said, they're just simple guys getting caught up in the system, the graft and bribery and shakedown and getting along the way you're expected to. But if they did it to me . . .

"Still, the militant way is not my way. For one thing, I can't afford it. I've got sixteen years invested in the Air Force. It's been my life.

"But I know things are changing. The new thing is that the old field niggers are suddenly coming to the fore. In the slave days, there were house niggers, the ones who worked directly with the white master, the slaveowner. B.N.I.C., they were called. Big Nigger in Charge. They kept the other slaves in tow and they informed on them, the troublemakers. They had the inside track, they got the leavings from the table. And the house girls, they had sheets on the bed and they slept with the white man. But the field niggers, they got the end of the shaft and they suffered and were beaten and nobody cared nothing about them. Now, they're all up North, and a hundred years later they're not about to take that any more."

However turbulent was this Bedford-Stuyvesant incident to its victims, and despite all of Vina's efforts to the contrary, there was no mention of it in any of the Monday newspapers except a brief note in the Harlem-based *Amsterdam News*. The *Daily News* made much of another beating wherein a plainclothes cop, patrolling as a decoy to draw muggers on New York's upper West Side, was himself mugged by three youths who took him for a drunk and got away with it. There was a feature story in the *New York Times* on the appointment of John Doar as executive director of a corporation set up to redevelop the Bedford-Stuyvesant section of Brooklyn, ". . . one of two such corporations founded by Senator Robert Kennedy, all part of a pioneering effort to regenerate the economic life of the community," that had begun with a $7 million federal grant six months before.

The *Times* also reviewed a TV show on the Negro soldier in Vietnam—"Same Mud, Same Blood": "Under battle tensions, racial antagonism is eradicated. A Negro soldier enjoys an equality of acceptance he is not likely to find at home."

For several days, the *Times* had been covering a controversy between Mayor John Lindsay and the Police Benevolent Association. Lindsay had opposed adding to the 28,228-man police force, while Norman Frank, then spokesman for the PBA, insisted that 5000 more policemen were essential to the security of the people of New York City. Said Frank: "The single most important subject on the lips of every citizen is crime in the streets. The Mayor tells us we must prepare for across-the-budget increases in almost every area of government. Yet in the area most important to the people, he tells us additional police are not required."

The *Times* commented editorially on the Mayor's suggestion to replace desk-bound policemen with civilian employees: "The wisest procedure is to get more patrolmen out on the streets. . . . There is no substitute for the visibility of the police. It discourages criminals and reassures the public."

9

There is not a shred of affluence in the Manhattan law offices of Conrad Lynn. For all its busyness, the building itself, on lower Broadway just south of Canal Street, has the smell of struggle and defeat in its old, cramped rooms. There is none of the high-style midtown money in this neighborhood. Luncheon business is not conducted in spacious gourmet restaurants but in over-crowded, tacky lunchrooms. These are the legal centers of the poor.

The four Blutchers were sitting there in their winter coats, fill-ing his little reception area with their dour presence, when Lynn returned from court sometime just after noon on that Monday. In the drama of his current work, he had almost forgotten this appointment. A black youth named John H. Prince, Jr., had re-quested non-combatant service on moral grounds while pending induction into the armed forces. An all-white draft board in Bed-ford-Stuyvesant had refused that request. He had been indicted, tried three times, for the first two juries had been hung, and the third had returned a guilty verdict. Prince was to receive the maximum sentence of five years of hard labor, and Lynn had been fighting it.

"Yes, there they were, waiting for me, sitting there like statues. Two men, two women. The women would do the talking, I knew. The men got beat up and the women did the talking. It was the way of black people in the ghetto."

"He looked so small," Vina thought. "I didn't expect that. It was sort of disappointing at first. He was wearing one of those Russian black fur hats and a little gray beard, his shoes needed a shine and he seemed shabby. I didn't know what to think. I guess I expected something different."

"He was a strong man," James Smith said, having come across Lynn in the course of a murder trial in Brooklyn a year or so before, then hearing him speak at a black protest rally. "He was an important man. I knew if he would take the case, it would be a good thing for Larry. We went out and scraped together a hundred dollars as a retainer, but I didn't know if he would take the case. He was really a very busy lawyer."

Lynn was, perhaps, busier than was good for him. For years, he had suffered an asthmatic condition that sometimes stripped him of his seemingly boundless energies, and he was not always able to perform the countless services inspired by his ardor. Yet his career is rich with an assortment of dramatic cases that is the stuff of fascinating history. In his thirty-five years as an attorney, Lynn's work had consisted of a doggedly militant defense of diverse and bizarre clients—the Puerto Rican Nationalists who sought world attention to their cause by wildly shooting up the House of Representatives in Washington, D.C.; the nine-year-old black child in North Carolina who was jailed for kissing a little white girl; Robert Williams, a Black Nationalist leader, author of *Negroes with Guns,* accused of kidnapping two whites during a KKK-inspired riot in Monroe, North Carolina, subsequently fleeing to Cuba and then to China; the Harlem Six— youthful defendants accused of murder in 1964—a case that

Lynn likened to the famed Scottsboro Case in the 1930s. Persistently active in politics as well, he was one of the founders of the Freedom Now Party, an attempt to rally black voters toward political power. Recently he had become expert in draft counseling, having written a book, *How to Stay Out of the Army—a Guide to Your Rights Under the Draft Law,* putting in print much of his current practice in this area.

"I grew up in Rockville Centre, Long Island, where my father had been a garbage collector—which, even to blacks, is considered the lowest of employment. Later he shifted to the more respected trade of landscape gardener. I remember, once, he took me to the huge dump at Scotic where the garbage was disposed of. It was a sprawling, foul-smelling mass of refuse, but over 300 blacks lived there in a community of primitive shacks. I was only a boy but I could never forget the sight of it. Years later, one of my first cases as a criminal lawyer involved a young Scotic black who had shot a neighbor in a quarrel over a woman. In my defense of this young man I described to the court what that place was like, and I accused the local lily-white jury of permitting its existence. Oh, they found the man guilty, but it swayed them to recommend a light sentence. The defendant was so moved by the essence of my plea that he wrote me a letter from prison telling me it had changed him as a man. Well, that was something. Scotic had changed us both."

(In recent years, Scotic had been purged of its filth and turned into a tree-lined community of 1200 lower-middle-class blacks. It was renamed Lakeview.)

Lynn was born in 1908, in the ultra-fashionable town of Newport, Rhode Island, where, at the time, his father was a coachman for August Belmont. "He was a faithful retainer, serving the rich . . . a classically inspired Republican, and he inflated his ego with a backhanded contempt for the poor, especially the white trash of Georgia that had been part of his heritage. My mother was a mulatto with a West Indian background, a descendant of the Grechies from Sea Island, just off the Georgia coast.

When things went bad up in Newport after World War I, when all the New England textile industries moved South for cheap labor, my father moved us all to Long Island."

Conrad Lynn was the first black to graduate from Malvern (Long Island) High School and the only one in his class to go to college. He was sent to Syracuse University by the white Mother's Club Scholarship Committee to reward his scholastic achievements. "Originally, I was going to be a minister, as my father wanted me to be, but the logic of my reading and studying took me from the philosophies of Kant through Hegel and Marx, and I switched from religion to law. But that was nothing compared to what happened when I joined the Communist Party in the thirties: my father wanted to throw me out of the family, but my mother prevented it. I worked hard for the Party (my first case was the Scottsboro Case), but the irony was, it was the Party who threw *me* out in 1937."

On the night of December 3, 1967, Lynn was at home with his family, having spent the dreary wet day in his bathrobe, working, reading, occasionally watching the commentary shows of Sunday TV. The anguished call from Brooklyn relating the beating of Laurence Blutcher was typically depressing—attorneys are accustomed to them the way doctors are always hearing of their patients' illnesses—and when he hung up, he made no mention of it to his family. He barely knew the caller, James Smith, and at first had trouble placing him. There seemed little promise of meaningful victory, and certainly none of sizable remuneration. If he took the case, it would be primarily out of a sense of duty to a victim. Lynn had recently become involved in a strange and somewhat comparable case: a young Puerto Rican, a carpenter's assistant, was riding to work in the morning subway rush, when a wood-carving tool he carried in his jacket pressed hard against his ribs. In an attempt to change its position, he exposed the knife and his hand brushed against a white woman standing beside him. At the next stop, the youth was pulled off the train by a plainclothesman who happened to have seen the episode, and was arrested. The bewildered woman, herself intimidated by the police, was instructed to charge the youth with attempted assault, and so it stood when it was brought to Lynn's attention.

"In a culture of violence, the law is not a gentle thing," Lynn speculated. "I had not committed myself to taking the Blutcher case, I told them that on the phone, but when I met them, I was immediately impressed by their poise and solidarity. It would seem that the victim was no ordinary black in the ghetto, but a young man of some ambition and initiative. It was a rare thing to come across a black who sought to run his own store. He was even more unique in his refusal to make payoffs. I liked the All-American middle-class ethic surrounding the story. Wasn't this young man practicing the very thing that the white man's culture always preached? And was he now to be punished for those very attributes?"

They could offer him the $100, all they could manage on short notice, promising the balance of $400 later. The Blutchers could only speculate on how much easier it might have been if Larry had paid the three-dollar shakedown.

("You can't beat City Hall," the police had derided the hand-cuffed youth at the Precinct, twenty-four hours before.)

"He was just trying to make an honest living," Mrs. Epsie Blutcher sighed.

"I'll take your case," Lynn smiled at them, but he could make no promise of victory. He instructed them about the difficulties involved. Witnesses, he told them. They must be sure to get witnesses, secure them. It must be impressed upon them how much Larry's case depended on them, that they would be called up to testify, and that, without them, it would be merely the defendant's word against that of the police.

They understood. They were extremely happy for his involvement. And for sister Vina, there was another valuable mission to perform.

Later that afternoon, Vina was back at Lafayette Avenue "with my hot little pen in hand." Her first target was Beverly Harris, the lady who lived across the street from Larry's store. From her window, she had a clear view of 960. What had she seen? Vina wanted to know. Exactly what had she seen? Mrs. Harris told her, not sparing details, the brutal sight of the two cops dragging out the handcuffed body, the way he was bleeding and all, and how they kicked and punched him into the car though he could barely move. Vina wrote it all down, word for word, just as the witness had described it, and then she had Mrs. Harris sign the paper, swearing that this was, indeed, the very truth of her experience.

And so it was with Bernard Trotta and his eleven-year-old son, Dexter. They, too, told her all they had seen, and fixed their signatures on the bottom of their statements.

And they all agreed that they would so testify in court, whenever it was asked of them. They would do what they could as eyewitnesses to this brutality so that justice could come to Larry Blutcher and the police who had beaten him. They heartily concurred that they must all stand firmly together in order to resist the onslaught of more and more police pressure.

Medically, it became clear by Monday noon that Larry Blutcher was going to survive the beating, but his appearance was even more ghastly than the evening before. His head was puffed up like a melon, the entire left side of his upper face a sinister-looking blue from internal hemorrhaging. The area around his left eye was so swollen the eye itself was not visible.

When his mother and his sister Tiny came to see him, he was still manacled to the bed. He spoke to them, trying hard to smile, as if it were his function to reassure them. His voice was barely audible and his words slurred from one to another. "I'm all right, momma, they're taking good care of me."

Larry had spent that Sunday night in the twilight zone of pain, floating in and out of sleep and consciousness, his mind vacillating between fear and relief, fantasy and reality. There were moments when, for all the drugs, his head throbbed with an unbearable pain, and he relived the terror of Repaci's pistol smashing down on him, re-hearing the hard crunch of iron on his skull with such vividness, he cried out like a child in a nightmare. It was not until he saw the light of Monday morning that he got a true fix on his survival. He lay on his bed and submitted to his pain, not thinking about anything now, barely conscious of his manacles, even, not knowing what was in store for him, caring only that he would live through it, whatever it was. He spent several days like this, a vegetable, sipping water and breathing. And then he began to get well.

Vina tried hard to keep the pressure up, maintaining a steady barrage of phone calls to city officials, to the Civilian Complaint Review Board. But time passed and Larry recovered, mitigating the power of her protestations. The hospital, for example, tightened up on visitation privileges, limiting the number of passes and visitors, "asking for all kinds of identification, red-taping the process so it took you as long to get a pass as it did to get there. . . . Then, a few days later, the police went to work in the neighborhood like they were out to stamp out a crime wave. They began to pick up everyone around for any infringements they could dream up: policy, civil disturbance, ticketing parked cars no matter whether they were there legally or not. They let it be known that they were going to be tough, like they were punishing the neighbors for even considering any protest demonstrations against them. Then they went right up into the apartments, up and down Lafayette Avenue—not the police from the Civilian Complaint Review Board as I had requested—the police without their badges on so you couldn't take down their numbers, yet making sure you saw the 79th Precinct button on their collars. They'd talk to the people in a way designed to scare them half to death. 'Are you on welfare, Mrs. Jones? I imagine you want to stay on welfare, now, wouldn't you? Now, did you see anything happen at the store on 960 Lafayette last Sunday? We're just trying to find out what happened, that's all. . . .'

Sure, and they found out that nobody saw anything, not a thing, at least nothing they were going to report. And the next thing I knew, Beverly Harris, who had seen plenty, had moved out of the neighborhood and left no forwarding address whatsoever."

Larry's recovery was strong and steady. It was not without irony that as he regained his health and was physically able to move around, the police released him from his manacles. He was moved to an adjacent room, 444, which he shared with another, and from there into the ward room and the company of many.

"The policemen on guard in the ward and the medics were very nice to me. Later they told me I was a good guy and gave them no trouble. In fact, they said they couldn't understand how I ever got into trouble in the first place. I told them I couldn't understand much how it happened either.

"There were other patients there who were really something. The stories they told about what the police did to them! One was a guy who had just picked up some drugs from a pusher when the police spotted him, and when he saw them, he started to run, and they shot him in the leg. He said they kept shooting as he lay there, he heard the bullets ricochet off the street a few feet from him, and he thought they were going to kill him, even though he was just lying there. Then there was a lady in the woman's ward, she was fighting to stay alive. She'd been riding in a taxi driven by a moonlighting cop, and he'd shot her six times, nobody really knew why. I heard later that the cop said she was a hooker and tried to hold him up, but she never did have a gun. The way she told it, the cop propositioned her and when she turned him down, he got mad and shot her. She was lying in the street and he kept on shooting. He put six bullets in her. A woman. And she'd never been a hooker at all!

"It was the ghetto in that ward. Black patients with the marks of violence all over us. Yet it was peaceful there. You were there to rest and heal, that's all. You lay on your bed and you talked. They brought you food and clean sheets and you let time and nature and the drugs mend you. And if you were inclined to, you had plenty of time to think.

"That's what I did, mostly. Think and read. I thought, how did I ever get in here with my head crunched in like this? The way I saw it, there had to be some sort of explanation, something more than what I knew. Like something must be wrong with my whole life. Something wrong inside my head. I saw my mother was crying and I felt sad for her, but I knew the answer to everything was not with her way. The whole world was all mixed up and here was one black man at the bottom of the mixer with nothing to show for his thirty years but a busted head and a string of failures.

"What did it all mean, all this, all the talk in that ward? I knew there was something to be learned from it, there had to be, there was so much that had happened to us all. The way I saw it, a man could get an education in that ward. A man could learn a lot about the U.S.A. he could never learn at Harvard. I mean, about how the system works to a black man. A man could get his Ph.D. on one of those beds.

"It's strange the way something can work its way into your head and suddenly everything is different. It's like the cartoon of the light bulb going on in your mind. For the first time, you see everything clearly. I don't know exactly when or how it happened to me. I guess the bug had been there for a long time and it just finally popped open. But in that hospital I came to a big conclusion about a lot of things, and especially about myself. I'd been a fool. I'd always been a fool. I'd been brought up to become a fool. It wasn't my parents' fault, they just didn't know any different. But no one ever really told me what it meant to be a black man, not so I had understood it, anyway. A black man, whether he likes it or not, whether he admits it or not, is a different man than a white man. And he can be one of three distinct types:

"He can be a hard-nosed black man playing the white man's

game, trying to get a little piece of the white man's action. Or he can, like most blacks, be a Tom, ready to do anything the white man tells him to do, just to stay in good with him. Or, he can be a man in the Third World, separate from the whites and the Toms where he can be independent in spirit and action, and he can learn to live with pride in his blackness.

"I remember how—it wasn't but a few years ago—I was walking down Lexington Avenue and I met this old buddy of mine called Abdul. He was called Butch when I used to know him, but now it was Abdul. He called me 'Tom.'

" 'What are you calling me Tom for?' I said.

" 'Look at yourself, trying to look like a white man, all dressed up like a white man, trying to get your hair unkinky and all . . .'

" 'I'm doing all right,' I said.

" 'You call that doing good? You put a clean shirt on and you think that's aces. You probably spending more money on your clothes than you are on eating. You can't make a life doing that, not on some lousy sixty a week. Man, the white man don't care about you, but all you is doing is what he wants you to do.'

"Well, that dented me some, but I didn't go out and quit my job or change my name to X. In fact, I didn't do much of anything. I just kept on doing what I'd been doing because I didn't know what else to do. I just kept right on going, that's all, not thinking, just taking it, whatever happened. I took it. I took it until they came and beat me over the head. . . .

"In the hospital, I began to see how you have to think of yourself as a complete man. You've got to act like a man, you've got to do more than just talk like one. I listened to some of those guys in the ward, and they made like being a man was just being tough, or taking whatever they wanted from anyone, stealing things, that being a man was just being defiant. I was seeing through that. What they were doing was playing at being a man without really trying to be one. That was the black man's problem. He couldn't see himself as a man because he only saw himself the way a white man sees him: You got a job? How much money you making? What house you live in? What kind of clothes your wife wear? I mean, if a black man can drive around in a shiny new Caddy, another black man will say, now ain't he something. A man is being judged, and judging himself, on what he owned and it didn't matter how he got it. The trouble was, he had to get it the white man's way, in the white man's system, and he had to play the white man's game all the time he was doing the getting. It had to be his whole thing. He couldn't be black and he couldn't be a man."

While Larry was in the hospital, his brother John kept an eye on the store and brought him the mail, such as it was. "Trouble mail," as Larry would call it: somebody selling something, and somebody trying to collect on it. The bill that made him laugh and cry was the monthly notice about payment for the new cash register. He'd missed one payment and the company was already screaming with threats about legal action. Larry turned it over to Frederick Douglass and forgot about it. Meanwhile, John and Larry's ex-partner, James Blakely, returned to the store with a photographer and took pictures of the mess caused by the beating, anticipating their possible use as evidence.

The day after, the store was robbed.

"I thought, wow, this mess is really going on and on. It really shook me up at first. They stole everything that was worth stealing, John told me: cigarettes, some canned stuff, and the new cash register with the eighty dollars in the secret compartment. Who did it? I guess you always wonder about that, but you know they're not going to catch them. In the black community, they don't catch a thief unless it's right in the act. Blacks steal from blacks because they know that the white police don't give a damn. The black man in the ghetto steals because he's poor, because the cops steal from him, because nothing is ever done about it. I mean, how many black people are going to tell a white cop about another black man who stole something? If they did, the white cop would probably think he's lying to cover up something. They'd suspect him. Look what happened to that dumb kid George Whitmore: he told a cop what he saw and the next thing, they almost had him in the electric chair for murdering those two white girls up near Park Avenue.

"Mostly, though, I didn't care about it much. I was in the hospital to get well, and the outside world seemed too far away. The store was like something I knew a long time ago, and after a while, I thought about it like it was someone telling me about an old girl friend I hadn't seen in years and she was going with another guy.

"Well, I guess it took some knocks on my head to drive something *into* my head. Oh, I knew it was working on me. I knew I must've been getting some sense. I knew it because of what happened when my wife, Jacqueline, came to see me.

"She walked into the ward and she told me she just flew down from Boston, she had heard about what had happened to me, saying she was my long-devoted wife or something like that. She stood beside my bed, looking so big-eyed and sad, those same sad eyes that had grabbed me from the first. She stood there with her coat on, and I said, well, why don't you take off your coat, and she smiled and said, no, I've got a surprise for you. Just like a wife. Anyway, finally she takes her coat off and there's her stomach sticking out, big as a basketball. Wow, I thought, what's this! She says, well, it's my surprise. This is your baby!

"Man, I shook and shuddered. Not again! I mean, I hadn't seen her in six months, not since that day she popped in at the store, and now she tells me this. She says she wanted to get back with me, that we could make it together, and all that lovey-dovey stuff. I said we'd better wait to decide anything until I got out of the hospital, but I knew this wasn't for me. If I went back with her, it would be like starting all over again, just the way it had been before.

"One thing I knew for sure: I wasn't about to have any more of *that*."

10

On December 15, after twelve days of hospitalization, Larry Blutcher was released, only to appear in police court with his attorney, Conrad Lynn, where he was charged with resisting arrest, felonious assault on a police officer, and given a summons for violating the Sabbath Law. Pending a hearing, he was dismissed without bail on his own recognizance. Apparently, Lynn's presence contributed to this first legal victory. It was only the beginning of a long legal battle of many phases and forms.

Lynn had been doing some initial digging, and in the process established his presence. A visit to the 79th Precinct in Brooklyn on Tuesday, December 5, just two days after the incident, and a conversation with Captain Charles Henry, a bright and personable Negro who was in charge. Just what were the charges against my client going to be, Captain? A routine interview, all very professional, but it showed that Blutcher would have some strength behind him.

The trouble was—and Lynn knew it—any show of strength

would bring about an immediate counter-action by the police. Whenever the police sense a threat to their integrity, they will raise the ante and attack all the harder. As noted, they had set the charge as high as they could: felonious assault on a police officer. In addition, Lynn was not surprised to learn, they had done some exploratory visiting in the neighborhood, two by two, badges removed to avoid identification and be all the more threatening, trying to find out exactly who had seen what, and in the process, leave a few suggestive hints that it would be a lot wiser to have seen nothing. Obviously, they had learned of witnesses who were prepared to testify. . . .

The pattern of such cases had long since been established. A police officer uses force—for whatever reasons, with whatever justification—and then charges the victim with assault to justify his violence. Most of the victims (black) are too poor to hire competent counsel. Their cases seldom get to trial. As it turns out, they seldom wish it to get that far. Neither, in fact, do the police nor the District Attorney who prosecutes. In almost all cases, a deal is arranged to avoid this: it is called plea-bargaining. The defendant is told he can plead guilty to a lesser charge of assault, a felony reduced to a misdemeanor, and in doing so, will be given a suspended sentence. It is a compromise solution that grants the victim his release and the police their innocence. The compromise, then, is achieved by way of the severity of the original charge—much like the houseowner who, wishing to sell for $20,000 will set his opening price at $25,000.

There is no official statistic to show the extent of this practice, though it is estimated that over 90 per cent of such cases are settled this way, avoiding a lengthy, time-consuming struggle in the overcrowded courts. If the victims have unfairly received a bloodied head, nature has a way of healing most wounds.

Paul Chevigny, an attorney for the American Civil Liberties Union, spent several years in defense of such victims and has documented his confrontations with these abuses in his book, *Police Power*.

The pattern seems to show that any action which raises the threat of a major case will cause the police to take steps to protect themselves. Defense lawyers generally regret the appearance of witnesses or the threat of a complaint before the trial . . . for the same reason they dread publicity. All these tend to make the charges more serious and the opposition more persistent.

Lynn, however, had no such regrets. In fact, this was exactly what he wanted. He had explained the plea-bargaining process to his client and Blutcher had rejected it. "Mr. Lynn, I didn't do any of those things they are charging me with. I didn't assault those cops, I didn't make a single move. If I had, you could bet they would've killed me right there in the store. And I didn't resist the arrest. I said to them, 'Okay, arrest me. Let's go to the Precinct.'" Blutcher wanted to fight the case, right through to the end. He wanted to right the wrong that had been done to him. He didn't care about the consequences if he lost. This being so, Lynn knew that the severity of the charges could then be turned against the District Attorney and the police, for it would be *their* burden to prove in court that the defendant had, beyond a reasonable doubt, assaulted those police officers.

It was the kind of fight Lynn could enjoy. If the cards fell properly, it was even possible to win it. In fact, Lynn regarded it all with a certain optimism, though he did not delude either himself or his client as to their chances. He liked Blutcher. He liked the forthright, honest, hard-working symbol of the victim. Here was a man who had played the game according to the white man's rules only to be beaten down by the referee. Yet he maintained a faith that his innocence would be rewarded, that the same system that had brought him to this point would reverse itself and bring him justice.

The action began a few days after his release from the hospital. On January 9, 1968, Blutcher and Lynn appeared before Police Court at Schermerhorn Street, Brooklyn, to answer the summons for violation of the Sabbath Law. It was to be the first of a dozen appearances, with Lynn present, brought about by his plea of not guilty. One could draw a parallel with the difficulties of making the same plea to a routine traffic violation: the police courts simply do not appreciate such controversy, nor is the machinery ready for it. The delaying game had begun.

Lynn saw the implications. It was all of a piece. If Blutcher was not in violation of the Sabbath Law, what were the police doing in his store in the first place?

He had referred to the law itself and read the specifics. In General Business Law, the Sabbath Law had long been on the New York State statute books, its origin inspired by the power of the Church, its history in the mores of the Bible: Sunday was to be cherished as a day of rest and prayer. All businesses were to be closed. Gradually, however, the law was amended to permit the opening of certain businesses and recreations considered essential to the public welfare, many of these the result of powerful lobbies for special interests. Included therein were food stores; Section 9 of the Law, applied to Larry Blutcher and the L&S Food Store, was as follows:

All manner of public selling or offering for sale of any property on Sunday is prohibited, except as follows:

1. Articles of food may be sold, served, supplied, and delivered at any time before 10 A.M.

2. Meals may be served at any time. . . .

3. Caterers may serve at any time. . . .

4. Prepared tobacco, bread, milk, eggs, ice, soda water, fruit, flowers, confectionery, etc., may be sold and delivered at any time of the day.

5. Grocers, delicatessen dealers and bakers may sell, supply, serve, and deliver cooked and prepared foods between the hours of four o'clock in the P.M. and 7:30 in the P.M. in addition to the time provided in subdivision one hereof, and elsewhere than in cities and villages having a population of 40,000 or more, delicatessen dealers, bakeries, and farmers' markets or roadside stands selling fresh vegetables or other farm products

may sell, supply, serve, and deliver merchandise usually sold by them, any time of the day.

The immediately applicable section was Subdivision 4. According to what Blutcher had told him, no meats or poultry had been sold during the few minutes he had been open prior to his confrontation with the police. He had done very little business on that early afternoon. Several packages of cigarettes, a few cartons of milk, a few loaves of bread. And, not without a drama of its own, a pickle. It was a matter of interpretation as to whether a pickle was in violation since the issuing of the summons had begun prior to its sale.

Lynn could only speculate on how many grocery stores were open on Sundays in all parts of the state where one could freely buy, at any hour of the day, all manner of illegal foods from thick steaks to a jar of caviar, where the grocer survived the profitable day with something better than a broken head to show for the violation. It was one of those laws that was enforced purely at the whim of local precincts in New York City and seldom even noted in most areas outside of it. As a result, there was an appalling ignorance about the details of the law, readily understandable upon consideration of its frequently amended intricacies. What could or could not be sold—between which hours of the day—was something of a mystery to both law-enforcement agencies and the grocers themselves. It was typical of the police to ignore the amendments and to treat the opening itself as a violation. It was much simpler that way. Would anyone expect them to wait around until a customer purchased a package of bacon for his Sunday brunch?

If the Law can be quick to pass out a summons, it is seldom as quick to adjudicate a contest of that summons. The process becomes so cumbersome, even a determined and dedicated defendant is tempted to submit to that famous old adage: Pay the Two Dollars! Lynn and Blutcher resisted. Though there had been no indictment proceedings against Blutcher, this minor violation had to be challenged, and there began what appeared to be a series of time-consuming delays. Starting with January 9, Lynn and his client were repeatedly summoned before the courts: February 1, March 26, April 29, May 8, July 25, each time without resolution. Lynn could not get a judge to rule on the violation. Ten months had passed since the incident and absolutely no progress had been made toward any aspect of its resolution.

Suddenly, in October, Blutcher was called before the Brooklyn Grand Jury to determine what action should be taken on the police charges against him.

"It didn't last very long. I mean, there were McCole and Repaci, and they told their story, and then I got into the chair and I told mine. The jury asked me a few questions. It was nothing much. The only thing I remember was the question about my shades. They wanted to know why I was wearing glasses inside the dark room, like maybe I was trying to hide a guilty look or something. I explained that the beating gave me headaches. The shades made it easier on my eyes. That was all."

It was a quick and cold examination, one of 4000 that the four constantly working grand juries of Brooklyn face each year, some 3500 of which end up in indictments. Significantly, only 15 per cent of these cases get to trial.

Blutcher was indicted on three counts: two separate charges of assault (one felonious), and resisting arrest. The indictment number was 2502.

To Lynn, the criminal aspect of the battle was now joined. The problem of the Sabbath violation, however, was wearing him down. Indeed, if this had been a deliberate battle of attrition against him, it could not have been waged more effectively. Hard-pressed for time on his busy schedule, facing still another inexplicable and harassing delay, on October 21 and their ninth such visit to the Court, he finally advised Blutcher to plead guilty and pay the five-dollar fine.

It was an action he (and his client) would later regret.

When Larry was released from the hospital, he was as free to pursue his business and his personal welfare as any man. There were a few rather severe limitations on this freedom, however, the most troublesome being the physical damage that continued to plague him. Headaches recurred persistently, incapacitating him for periods of several hours. He was afflicted with dizzy spells in surprisingly sudden attacks, and when he recovered from them, he found his left hand and arm to be partially paralyzed. He visited a medical clinic for weekly examination and therapy, the substance of which was a prescription for Darvon, a pain-killer to be taken during headache spells.

Meanwhile, he returned his concentration to the store and the prospect of reopening, a job that began at the bottom. Much of the stock had been depleted through food spoilage and the robbery. He owed on rent, electricity, and random other debts, not the least of which was the $30 monthly charge for the cash register and meat slicer. The theft was doubly aggravating because of the $80 he had hidden in the secret compartment, and he wondered about its ever being discovered. The company made repeated calls, demanding payment, and Larry explained how he'd been beaten and robbed. "I told them I didn't have the cash register or the slicer any more. I was lying about the slicer, though: I'd taken that upstairs to use at a party in my apartment a week or so before the beating. I told them I couldn't pay the fee. I didn't have any money, that was all there was to it, and they could sue all they wanted.

"It was wild: the man on the phone seemed surprised about the meat slicer. 'The meat slicer is gone, too? I was told only the cash register was stolen.' When I hung up, I thought, wow, how did he know that? Who could've told him that? Nobody knew about the slicer being upstairs. Nobody. Then I thought, the only way they could know is that they must have been in on the stealing themselves!

"There were lots of problems with all the money that people

owed me, all that credit. I went around to their houses and asked for the money, but most of them, they gave me the stall. They just didn't have it, they said. I could tell that they weren't going to pay me, at least not until I could get the store open again. They all acted sorry for what had happened to me, but they didn't pay up. It was because they have to struggle so hard for what little they get; when they see someone who can't do them good any more, they don't want to truck with him. It ended up, they took me for over $150."

What became apparent to him was that he could not arrange for a reopening without a substantial loan. He went to the Restoration Corporation of Bedford-Stuyvesant, established under the aegis of Senator Robert Kennedy, working for the benefit of small businesses. "I went down there prepared with all sorts of statements from bookkeepers and all, all my needs were listed, and with letters of recommendation, the works. I wanted a $5000 loan. I wanted to fix up everything and fill the shelves. I thought, the only way I would open this time would be the right way.

"But they told me, No. No loans to grocery stores, shoeshine parlors, beauty parlors. There's been too many losses in that type of store. But the man there suggested, how would I like to own a milk-jug place? The Sunnydale Dairy Company was giving out franchises. I would run a chain store that sells milk products at cheap prices. The man was a black brother, a former teacher, and he convinced me it might be a fine idea. And when I couldn't get a loan for my store, it seemed it might be a very good thing if I went along with this. He took me around to see some of these milk-jug places, picked me up in his car, even.

"So I sold the L&S Food Store. All I could get for it was $700. I owed $450 to my ex-partner, James Blakely, and the rest I gave to my sister Vina to repay some of what she had loaned me. And that was the end of it. Two years of hard work. I didn't envy the guy who took it over, even at the bargain price he paid for it.

"The trouble was, the Sunnydale deal never came through.

They told the brother that there would be no franchise in Bed-ford-Stuyvesant. They had investigated and decided it would not pay them to invest in any business there. So it turned out that I was left with nothing."

Not long after, fifty mortgage bankers met for a luncheon in the Waldorf-Astoria Hotel where they were told by a Negro banker, Dempsey J. Travis, that black-owned businesses were fewer in number than forty years ago, "despite press releases being churned out around the country that might lead one to believe the opposite. It seems that the development of black capitalism within any period—dating back to the post-Civil War days—has depended greatly on the mood and climate of the power structure." As reported in the *New York Times,* he called on the federal government to be "consistent in matching rhetoric with deeds and not to provide opportunities and then take them away."

Shortly thereafter, Howard J. Samuels, the recently fired head of the Small Business Administration, accused the Nixon Administration of failing to support loans to minority-owned businesses, allowing a backward slip of 20 per cent "when such aid is a major tool in rebuilding inner cities. . . . The federal government seems to have moved away from the principles of 'compensatory capitalism,' a new premise holding that higher risks are acceptable when high-priority social and economic objectives are at stake."

Samuels was overstating his protest: it had never been otherwise. As far back as three years before—as Blutcher more recently learned—it was SBA policy that loans could be made only 'when there was a reasonable assurance of repayment,' thereby setting up an infuriating cycle of frustration. If the SBA could refuse a desperate ghetto loan because the risk seemed too great, the banks obviously would have no need for the SBA in the first place. Then, too, they issued that ruling excluding grocery stores "and other businesses of the types traditionally operated by members of disadvantaged groups unless there is a clear indication that such businesses will fill an economic void in the community." As Theodore Cross points out in his book *Black Capitalism*, "The feeble and segregated personal service establishment, sustained only by freedom from white competition, is often the only route open to the fledgling black businessman."

Cross refers to a feature story on Senator Robert Kennedy's Restoration Corporation, designed to help develop new business in Bedford-Stuyvesant, and a businessman's reaction toward any such program in the ghetto. "Senator, the afternoon I walk into my Board of Directors and tell them Bobby Kennedy was here today and thinks we should put a plant in Bedford-Stuyvesant is the afternoon they will have me committed."

It was the same all over. "The economic failures of America's slums," Cross writes, "are so massive that industry as a whole has neither the capability nor the will to impair its capital or earnings to the degree that is necessary to revise the crushing forces of profitlessness and risk that the separate slum economy has built and nourished over a period of many years."

As Blutcher, the victim, would put it: "The only money around is welfare money. The neighbors buy on credit and I have to wait for the checks to come in. They say, what money there is comes into the ghetto at 9 A.M. and goes out at 5 P.M. It's all white man's money, and you can be sure he takes out more than he brings in."

On December 15, 1967 (the day Blutcher was released from the hospital), the *Wall Street Journal* reported that for all the government effort after the bitter riots of 1965 to stir ghetto business in Bedford-Stuyvesant, only 600 new jobs had been created.

Cross goes on to note how the problem compounds: "In recent years, with national Negro unemployment running twice as high as whites, Southern Negroes are no longer seeking jobs, but rather higher welfare benefits in Northern cities." There are, for example, ghetto blacks who do not own alarm clocks because they never have to be any place at any particular time.

Meanwhile, there remain a majority of those who endorse the classic American businessman's attitude that, if a man is healthy and out of work, he must be lazy.

Larry Blutcher was left out in limbo. "I didn't know what to do. My headaches were not getting better. Worse, in fact. My eyes would hurt at any bright lights and bring on even more headaches. I took more Darvon, just like they told me to do at the clinic. They said there was nothing else they could do for me. Months went by and I started to worry about it. My family, they were all worried. I could tell the way my mother would call, or the way she looked at me. Everybody thought there must be something wrong with me because I wasn't getting any better.

"Then, one morning, I was going out and got an attack of the dizzy thing just as I stood on the landing. I tried to hold onto the wall, but everything turned on me and went spinning. And the next thing, I went tumbling down the flight of stairs, maybe ten steps down. That's when everyone got scared. But the doctors kept telling me that it was just temporary, that I'd get over it. There was nothing to do but let time do the healing.

"It was a real bad time for me. Like I was just hanging around waiting for the trial, not knowing when I was going to get well or get tried. I couldn't get a job or go to work because of both those troubles. Nobody wants a sick black man who has to take time off all the time to run back to court. They'd fire him in a minute.

"What I did mostly was read and paint. I started to paint pictures, something I always wanted to do. I set up an easel in my living room and I'd paint what I saw in the streets or what I pictured in my head. I had to learn how to use the brush, how to handle colors. At first, they were pretty sad, those paintings, but then I started to get a little better. I liked it very much because I began to feel what I was painting. I mean, it would get me excited, the way you get when someone is telling you something special and you feel for them. I'd paint and look at my work and get that way. Like *I* was telling something special."

Larry was also spending considerable time with his brother John's organization, Together We Stand. He would work with the children there on weekday afternoons, after their school day had finished, teaching painting and arts and crafts.

"I saw a lot more of Bubba than usual. What stood out to me was the way he was changing. Very serious, now. He was always carrying a book with him. He would talk about things, mostly about race. Not like someone who knew all the answers the way some blacks do. Bubba, he was thinking, asking questions, trying to learn. I guess I didn't help him too much. I'm not the philosopher type. I'm more the practical, the do-something type."

John Blutcher was doing something. His organization was growing rapidly, principally as a result of his energy and commitment. He ran the operation from a tacky store-front meeting room and office on the corner of Reid and Stuyvesant Avenues, two small rooms heated by a gas space-heater for which he paid $70-a-month rent. The front room, the meeting room, was about twelve by twenty feet, with thirty or forty folding chairs. On the wall, WE LEAD THE WAY BY STANDING TOGETHER the TWS poster proudly declared. Beneath it, it had a picture of a black boy and a blond white, with the TWS flag, a tricolor of blue, white, and yellow, representing the three leading races of the world. (The blue was supposed to be black, but no black cloth was available at the time of its making.)

"We stand for all good causes," reads the preamble.

"To keep the peace at all times, sir," recite the TWS children.

"To obey our mothers and fathers.

"To obey our teachers and all Enforcement Officers in the performance of their duties, sir.

"To keep our appearance neat and body physically fit at all times, sir."

In the back room, the office, John went through a daily confrontation with a myriad of typical community problems, relating to both kids and parents. "I guess the main problem for us is that more people want something from us than those who want to do for us. Still, we do okay. We used to be funded with government poverty money, but that ended in September 1968. Actually, sometimes I think it's better without it. We're more eager now. We self-help more. We involve the community directly, and I don't have to take orders from bureaucrats. If the community doesn't support us, we're dead. We do more for everyone that way, without government money or support, than other organizations do with a lot of it. Hell, I used to work for the OEO and I know. It's very bureaucratic, very cliquish. It got me off base. You tend to do everything by the book, very safe and all. You worry more about losing the funding than you do about the people you're supposed to be working for. The way I've learned it, all organizations should be self-supporting. If it can't come right out of the guts of the community, it shouldn't exist.

"The truth is, and everyone knows it, there's a greater need for this kind of organization than ever. In the neighborhood, things are getting so bad, so full of chaos, someone has to do something.

"The problem with the police is one thing. We work with them as much as possible. We're not against them. There's a war on with the police in Bedford-Stuyvesant. It's a quiet war, but it's there, under the surface. When they beat up Bubba, there was a time when you thought the people might go crazy in the streets. People who didn't hardly know him. It's very important that the community has something to say about the police in the neighborhood. We have to know what's ours to live with or else there's no pride in it. You don't fight a war with your own kind. You fight it with outsiders. The police, they're all outsiders. They're not allowed to live in the neighborhood. That's a police rule. I suppose that's good for the police, but it's bad for the neighborhood.

"TWS is just a beginning. We have to grow. We do little things, for the kids, mostly. Give them a feeling of respect and pride and discipline. We teach them what little we can. African studies. Arts and crafts. Carpentry. Gymnastics. Judo. We help them with their school work, remedial reading. What we're famous for is our drill teams. Twenty-one kids, eight-year-olds. Twelve-year-olds. They get all dressed up like flashy soldiers, and they drill; it's like a dance, really. They've been on TV, on the show "Inside Bedford-Stuyvesant." We even have a group of four-teen-to-eighteen-year-olds, the Rangers, we call them, and they cruise around to prevent muggings in the neighborhood.

"I dreamed of this organization one night. The name and all. I really dreamed it. Together We Stand. Like when momma dreamed that number back in Georgia, 210. I took my dream and went to work on it. It was the best thing I ever did in my life . . ."

It was good for Larry to be part of it. For the first time, he sensed the togetherness that had become the way of kids in the ghetto. He had grown up in the days of street gangs and chaos, and now kids were thinking about how they could make things better for everyone. The Dukes and Saints and Apostles had long since dissolved, the days of the big rumbles were gone, the neighborhood warfare was gone. Life in Bedford-Stuyvesant was as gruesome as ever, but things were changing. He could see it all around him. And most of all, he could see it in himself.

"From the time I was in the hospital, everything in my head was busted wide open. It was like this savage thing had happened to me and that I had to learn from it or something even worse would happen to me later. I was sure of it. I had to know something more about myself. There was something missing, I knew that. I guess I'd known it for a long time. Like how I really wasn't a man. I didn't act like a man. I'd be skipping around from one thing to another, from one woman to another. Most of all, I didn't believe in anything. I was brought up in Christianity, but it didn't mean a thing to me. I just didn't think about it any more. I'd been to school, been in love, did a hitch in the Army, gotten into trouble, had kids, even married. I'd done a lot of things, but it wasn't worth a thing, not a thing, not to myself, not to anyone.

"I caught hold of that thought. What was the matter with me? What was I supposed to do with the rest of my life?

"I guess all this had been stewing in my mind. I knew it was there, bubbling away when I was in the hospital. It was there before that, too. But now, it was all coming to a head. One thing I knew: I couldn't go on with the same thoughts. I needed to have faith in something so I could have faith in myself. And to do this, I had to figure out where it had all gone wrong.

"I began reading some things, and this time, I cared about what I read. I really sank my teeth in it. I read Malcolm X, about how he got religion in jail. I read "Message to the Black Men," that came from Elijah Muhammad. I started to read African history, the whole black heritage thing. I read Eldridge Cleaver, Frantz Fanon. It took me months because I wasn't in practice, but then I started to get the feel of reading. And it sunk in. It sunk in and it shook me up. I couldn't stop thinking about these things and then I came across other blacks who were thinking about it, too.

"What I came to realize was how completely we had been brainwashed to hate ourselves. How the white man had taught us that we weren't fit to be equals and that in all of history we were never worth anything. But when I read about Africa, I found out different. Blacks have got to go into their past to find out how we weren't always so helpless, so worthless, and then maybe we can have more confidence in ourselves. When you read history and find out we had once reached a higher level, we had made great achievements and contributions to civilization in arts and sciences and government, and when you know that you once did that, you think you can do it again.

"Most of us, all we ever see is the white man and his power. He seems like a giant. Next to him, we are just dogs. We are taught to hate our color, the kinky hair, the shape of our nose

and all. We end up, we hate ourselves. We're made to feel infe-
rior and helpless. That's why the white man has always painted
Africa as the primitive black continent so that we'd be ashamed
of our heritage. If we were ashamed of Africa, we'd be ashamed
of ourselves.

"All this I began to understand. I read how there were great
black civilizations in ancient times. How, once, they were the
greatest in the world. In fact, the first man was African and so he
was black. And then you start thinking that Jesus himself must
have been colored. I learned how the white man from the North
came down across the Mediterranean Sea and subjugated the
blacks, how they turned Africans against each other, divide and
conquer, and eventually made slaves of us in America.

"This was our history, but it was history I never learned in
school.

"What it came down to, the black man is really neither Christian nor American. Like Malcolm wrote: 'I'm not an American.
Being here in America doesn't make you an American. Being
born here doesn't make you an American. You wouldn't need
any amendments to the Constitution, you wouldn't be faced with
a civil-rights filibuster in Washington, D.C. They don't have to
pass civil-rights legislation to make a Polack an American. He's
an American the day he gets off the boat.' And Claude Brown,
he wrote: 'All this Christianity . . . what's it taught the blacks to
do? Nothing. Nothing that could benefit them. Just bow their
heads to Mr. Charlie, buy bleach creams, straighten their hair,
buy a Cadillac they can't afford, and follow some white, blond-
haired blue-eyed Jesus to a mythical place called heaven.'

"Even my mother, she began to listen to me. After what had
happened to me, she saw how maybe you've got to change your
thinking some. You can't keep on believing what the white man
tells you to believe. It gets you nowhere. I made her think about
that old-time religion she learned down South, how they used to
eat and drink and pray in the churchyard with that big white
Jesus looking down on them, how they were taught to have

faith in that sort of thing. I said to her, 'Momma, you gotta know that ain't where it's at. Praying to that is like praying to the white man. And you know how it's written in the Bible, that God created you in His image. Now how come He can be a white Jesus if that's so?' My momma, she heard me and she started to come around. She came to understand this whole new African thing, with blacks dressing like blacks, not like whites, and not slopping that hard grease on their heads to straighten their hair and all. She took her wig off and wore her hair natural, and she felt proud of herself. My momma and me, we're very close now.

"Then, in the summer, I met Monica Warnic. I was selling tickets to a raffle up in Times Square, raising money for TWS, and she was there, too. I'd known her sister before, but I never knew Monica. She sure looked beautiful. I mean, it was something extra to see her doing the same thing I was doing. I felt close with her right away. It was being together, standing in the street trying to get people to buy those raffle tickets. And right away, I knew that this was the kind of feeling a man is supposed to have when he knows what it's all about."

11

If Lynn and his client were impatient for the trial, the Criminal
Court of Brooklyn was not, apparently, in any comparable hurry.
Indictment #2502, People vs. Blutcher, had been assigned to Part
IX of the Supreme Court, Criminal Term, to be tried in the Supreme Court Building at the Civic Center when the indictment
number came up, much the same as a shopper's ticket number at
a crowded bakery. However, this is not the way it worked out
with 2502. The DA's office saw fit to bypass the Blutcher case,
and though Lynn was not immediately aware of it, cases with
higher numbers were given preference.

Then, on December 2, 1968, almost exactly one year after the
beating of Laurence Blutcher by Officer Philip Repaci, that same
policeman was on routine patrol in his squad car when he skid-
ded out of control and crashed, breaking his left leg in multiple
fractures from his ankle to his hip. For several weeks, it was
doubtful that the leg itself could be saved, and several months
before he could achieve any mobility.

As a result, it would appear that there could be no immediate disposition of People vs. Blutcher, since the principal witness for the prosecution was indisposed, but the court calendar did not respect that. On Friday, January 24, Blutcher was finally notified to appear for trial on the coming Monday. Conrad Lynn, similarly notified, instructed his client to see that his witnesses (especially the two Trottas, father and son) were alerted, that they must be ready to appear when needed, presumably on the second or third day when the defense would state its case. They prepared themselves accordingly. Neither Lynn nor Blutcher had, as yet, heard of Repaci's accident.

Blutcher spent his weekend thinking of little else. "I guess I didn't sleep very much on Saturday night. It was like that again on Sunday. But when I got to the courthouse, I felt calm. I sat on the spectators' bench and waited for Mr. Lynn while the judge was sentencing a young black man named John Something-or-other with hair conked and all. I could see he'd been on dope, but nobody said nothing about that. The white judge just bawled him out for being a punk and sent him away for two years, telling him how he was lucky it wasn't twice that much, after the robberies he'd been convicted of. The bailiff came and put the cuffs on him, and then it was bye-bye John.

"I couldn't help but think how that might have been me. I mean, my life had been so crazy, it just might have gone the wrong way. I thought of everything that had happened to me so far, how I had been taught to stay out of trouble, to be a good Christian and not do any wrong. I remembered how kids would push over trash cans and kick the garbage all over the street, then run away, how they'd steal some fruit from a stand, then run away, how they'd snap an antenna from a parked car, steal a purse from a lady, always running away. I was taught never to do that, that it was wrong to steal anything. But here I was, a defendant against the People of the State of New York, and nobody cared much about what I had done, like it was all the same, me and this guy John with the handcuffs on. I could just as well be him.

"I remembered when I finally did steal. It was one hot summer day and the ice cream truck was in the street, how we'd got the driver around one side of the truck so we could open up the back door and grab some pops. I didn't plan it, but I was in it. I took the ice cream and ate it, and it sure tasted good. It tasted so good, I couldn't sleep that night. I had sinned. I could feel the judgment of God on me. I never told my momma, I was too ashamed. It all seemed horrible, but after a while, it didn't seem so horrible. Stealing like that, when you didn't have any money, it got to seem like it was just something you did in the streets. It was part of being in poverty. It was part of growing up without knowing anything.

"Like this man John in court. He was my age, I could guess. Sure, he must've stolen ice cream, and maybe fruit and old ladies' purses, and when he grew up, he didn't have anything better to do, so he got to smoking grass, and then he was sniffing heroin, and then maybe he really got the habit, so he needed a hustle to support it. Then he gets a bad week so he does something crazy like stick up a gas station or a liquor store, and blam, here he is. It was sad, all right."

The clerk of the court called the next case, "People vs. Blutcher," his eyes scanning the room for its participants. Larry stood up, shaken, now, by the continued absence of his attorney.

"Are you Butcher?" the clerk asked, mispronouncing the name.

"Blutcher, yes, sir," Larry corrected him.

"Yes, Blutcher," the clerk repeated it, correctly this time. He even seemed apologetic about his error. "Your attorney, Mr. Lynn, is he here?"

Larry looked around, embarrassed by the absence and his inability to explain. He felt totally alone and abandoned. And then Assistant District Attorney Sheldon Greenberg interceded, explaining that he had been notified by Mr. Lynn of his inability to appear in court on that morning due to previous scheduling, requesting that People vs. Blutcher be postponed until the following day.

It was postponed two weeks until February 10. The clerk then delivered the official warning that Blutcher was to appear on that date under penalty of forfeiting his parole, adding an ominous, "Do you understand?"—sounding like a severe schoolteacher threatening a pupil who had a history of repeated tardiness.

Yes, Larry assured him that he understood, and at that, he was dismissed. It wasn't until he got back to his apartment that he discovered his phone had been out of order for two days: a telegram from Mr. Lynn, sent the day before, was waiting for him.

On February 10, Lynn was present with his client, but this time Assistant DA Greenberg was not. The court passed until further notification.

On Friday, February 14, Blutcher and Lynn again received notice announcing trial on Monday, the seventeenth. Again, Lynn instructed Blutcher to alert his witnesses. On that date, Assistant DA Greenberg was present and finally informed the court of Patrolman Repaci's accident. The judge nodded and marked the case off the calendar until further notice.

Both Lynn and Blutcher were stunned. It was all so sudden and so blandly revealed. Just how serious was the injury? How long was the anticipated period of hospitalization? A case marked off the calendar in this fashion would probably not be tried for four to six months.

Assistant DA Sheldon Greenberg had more practical ideas. He confronted Lynn in the hall and drew him aside for a private chat. There was no reason to take this case to trial, he informed Lynn. A deal was very much in order. The District Attorney would be willing to reduce the charge from a felony to a misdemeanor—a non-felonious assault—if the defendant would plead guilty. Greenberg would then arrange for a suspended sentence and the whole matter would be closed.

It was, of course, the routine maneuver, the opening round in the classic game of plea-bargaining. Lynn, however, was not inclined to participate, having long since been over the possibilities with his client. He agreed with Greenberg about one thing, however: he, too, felt there was no need to go to trial, and suggested that the whole matter could be resolved if the DA's office simply dropped the indictment. Greenberg was appalled at the brashness of such a request. Whatever he thought of Lynn's chances of winning, or even the merits of the People's case against Blutcher, it would be impossible for him to recommend such a resolution, for it left the police far too vulnerable—especially in consideration of any civil action the defendant might take against the city itself—if the assault charges would not hold up. In short, the DA needed a conviction or a plea of guilty. And that, too, was the very predictable norm.

So the two lawyers parted company, having resolved nothing but a demonstration of their opening positions. If Lynn was going to insist on a trial, the DA was going to demand a conviction. The defendant, meanwhile, was going to have to wait another interminable period before anything further happened.

Lynn, meanwhile, was concerned about the civil action. The law stated that such an action must be filed within fifteen months of the cause of the complaint, normally a sufficient time for the consummation of any criminal proceedings against the complainant. In this case, the terminal date was March 1, 1969, and no trial was immediately in the offing. Lynn had discussed this matter with the lawyer for the Blutcher family, Frederick Douglass, but that had been a year before. He called Douglass to remind him of the matter, a well-advised call, for no such action had yet been filed. With his client's permission, then, Lynn immediately did so himself. The City of New York would be sued for false arrest and criminal assault by the policeman upon the body of Laurence Blutcher, and pressed for damages amounting to $1 million.

It was a figure that both staggered and amused Larry. If he entertained any serious hopes of becoming wealthy through the legal process, Lynn was quick to disabuse him of it. It was highly unlikely that they would even get to trial, he explained. Civil actions were possible, yes, but they took endless years to prosecute and they were extremely costly. Whatever difficulties they might have in convincing a jury in the criminal action would be compounded many times over in a civil case. The jury, after all, consisted of taxpayers. The same twelve citizens who might well find Larry innocent of assaulting the policemen would probably be less sympathetic to his plight when it came to handing over taxpayers' money. Nonetheless, it was the only course open to Blutcher. It was the one way of fighting back, of righting the wrong inflicted on him. As Paul Chevigny pointed out: "Policemen prosecute citizens for assault as a matter of course, but I have yet to see a citizen take out a summons against a police officer for assault and get his case to trial." While many police abuses are, in fact, crimes (e.g., police brutality usually can be considered an assault, and, if serious enough, felonious assault) and, theoretically, prosecution by the DA is called for, still— unless a killing is involved—the DA does not prosecute. Discipline, if any, is left to the Police Department itself.

This was the avowed purpose of the famed and short-lived Civilian Complaint Review Board as established by Mayor John Lindsay in June 1966. General Order #14 had provided for a mixed board of four civilians and three police members. As pointed out by Algernon Black, who sat on that Board: "The purpose of the civilian majority was to overcome distrust by the public and to build more confidence that the complaints of civilians would receive more consideration than they had in the past. . . . It was hoped that the police would be more aware of the need to respect civilians and protect basic civil rights." It was also hoped that a workable machinery could be established that would lead to the proper disciplining of offending police officers.

The machinery devised was simple enough: the seven members would hear the complaints after an investigative and screening process (performed by a staff of forty police officers) recommended review. The Board would then vote its recommendation. The Review Board, it must be emphasized, had investigative and advisory power only; no judicial or disciplinary authority went with it. It was up to the Police Commissioner's discretion whether or not he would follow the Board's recommendation. "The Board would . . . in no way interfere with the Commissioner's power and responsibility to maintain discipline and control of the Police Department."

However, even within these grave limitations of power, the Civilian Complaint Review Board was condemned by the Police Benevolent Association as a threat to the Department. Even before the Board was appointed, the PBA had drawn up a petition to force a referendum—to exclude civilians from any such Board —to appear on the November ballot, just four months later. Immediately, a well-financed campaign was initiated to get the referendum approved, persuading the voters of New York City that such a Board tied the hands of the police, broke their morale, compromised their integrity, and stripped their power. ("Did you see the pictures of those riots, of Negro thieves running wild? And did you see the cops stand by, idly watching the debauchery? That was the result of a Civilian Complaint Review Board.")

The vote was a staggering two-to-one in favor of the PBA referendum, reflecting the frightened mood of the times. Riots, muggings, violence in the streets, armed robbery, civil rights, and anti-war demonstrations had set up a backlash that upset the balance of urban living and threw more and more power to the strictest interpretations of old-fashioned law and order. "Suppression" was to replace "permissiveness," demanding a return to a disciplined society. The morality of Chicago Mayor Daley's "Shoot to kill!" was considered preferable to any implementation of civil-rights laws. Crime was the enemy, and the police were to be given carte blanche to subdue it.

It was no surprise, then, that sister Earvina Blutcher's protest-

ing letter of December 3, 1967, to the Review Board, stripped of
its civilians and its public support, provoked no disciplinary action against the offending officers. Late in the fall of 1968, some
ten months after she had written her complaint, she received an
official reply from the Board:

CIVILIAN COMPLAINT REVIEW BOARD
POLICE DEPARTMENT, CITY OF N.Y.
200 PARK AVENUE SOUTH   AT 17TH ST.
NEW YORK, N.Y. 10003   TEL: 673-6001

Members of the Board:

Louis L. Stutman, Chairman

Abraham P. Chess   Bernard H. Jackson
Joseph T. McDonough   Executive Director

                                    September 19, 1968
                                    Re: CCRB No. 1179 (67)

Mrs. Earvina Blutcher
1687 St. John's Place, Apt. 12
Brooklyn, N.Y.
Dear Mrs. Blutcher:

Your complaint was received at the Civilian Complaint Review Board on the 3rd day of December, 1967. It was referred
to the investigative staff and a report was prepared. At a recent
meeting of the Board, that report was reviewed.

After a very thorough and impartial evaluation of the investigative report in this case, the Board was unable to find
enough objective and persuasive proof to substantiate the alle-
gations of your complaint. Obviously, such proof is required if
disciplinary procedures are to result from your complaint. This
is so in every disciplinary proceeding.

This letter is written to you by and under the authority of the Review Board and the Police Commissioner.

Very truly yours,
[*signed*]
Henry Weiner
Assistant Director
Civilian Complaint Review Board

Conrad Lynn spelled it out for his client: the times were bad. The forces that unleashed Repaci's gun would also be working in that jury box. Yet there was always the chance that they could win. He was ready to fight it out all the way—if Larry was prepared to take the consequences of defeat. With Larry's police record—those four arrests and convictions—Lynn explained that the judge would be forced to send him to jail, perhaps for as long as six months. Was Larry certain he was willing to take such a risk?

"A year ago I would've said no. I would've taken the soft way out. You cop a plea like the system tells you to, and you forget the whole thing. Only now I was different. I was changed. Mr. Lynn knew it. That's why he was so interested in the case and interested in me. I wasn't just another black sucker any more. I wasn't going to be another victim. I wanted to go on trial and make them face up to what they had done to me.

"The whole thing was, I was trying to be a man now. A black man; a black man is a special man, and I had a faith now to help me. A black man's faith it was, and I was proud . . ."

At the core was his developing attachment to the Nation of Islam, more conventionally known as the Black Muslims. He was uplifted by its demands upon him, the disciplines it imposed. He was proud of his cleanliness, the conservative neatness of his attire, the orderliness of his apartment. He found added strength in the purity of his new eating habits as specified by Elijah Muhammad, their leader, that emphasized the avoidance of such conventional black soul food as ham, pork, chitlings, beans, and shellfish. He liked the friendliness accorded to him by Muslim brothers and sisters when they met, the strict morality of their conduct. He saw broken men rallying toward living worthwhile, constructive lives. He saw others who had been hopelessly addicted to heroin taken off the streets and regenerated by the power of Muslim attentiveness and support. He saw hardened criminals reformed into brotherly men. He saw himself believing in something for the first time in his adult life, something that made sense out of the chaos.

As Elijah Muhammud put it: "Most Negroes think white. They are made to hate black. Islam teaches us to be ourselves, to love ourselves, our brothers and sisters; to act for ourselves, to stop being liars, being afraid; stop being the laughing stock of the world; to stop being children all our lives . . ."

Larry studied the religion of Islam, a religion of submission to Allah, God of the Worlds, embracing half a billion people from every continent, including every race of man. He studied the Quran (Koran), the message as delivered by the prophet Muhammud, and the words of hope and unity gave him strength: ". . . and hold fast, all of you together, to the cable of Allah, and do not separate. And remember how ye were enemies and He made friendship between your hearts so that ye became brothers by his Grace . . . And there may spring from you a nation who invite to goodness, and enjoy right conduct and forbid indecency." He would read it aloud, for it literally sung with poetic recitations that inspired him: "And we shall try you with fear and hunger, and loss of property and life and blessings; therefore, O Prophet, give good tidings to those who are patient . . . who, when misfortunes befall them say: verily we belong to God and to Him we shall verily return . . ."

Though he did not become an orthodox disciple—indeed, there were many who remained on the fringes of the movement —he felt the pull of a vast togetherness with his people. He saw himself as a new man. Like other blacks, he used to think of himself as ugly, he used to talk of leaving America for a place where a black man could live better than a dirty dog in the streets. Now, he could sense there was beauty in the struggle, and the world seemed different for it all.

Then, too, he had Monica who was also in the faith. He was in love in a way that deeply moved him. He was not just using a woman any more. He felt like a man ought to feel with a woman, and each gave the other's life a new meaning. Her beauty seemed to him to be complete. He would look at her and be awed by how lovely she was. He could see the trust by which she lived, knowing that much of it came from his own sense of honor, and it was joyous to both that they could give this to each other. He painted her portrait, trying to capture this glow, and though he was not up to doing her justice, he was moved by what little he had accomplished.

Monica spent her working hours as a secretary-typist at a large Manhattan insurance company, but at all other times, they were inseparable. And like all true lovers, he wondered what he had ever done without her.

Although Officer Philip Repaci remained in the hospital during the entire spring, Lynn and Blutcher were repeatedly summoned to appear for the opening of trial. They made five more fruitless trips to the Supreme Court building, only to be advised, each time, that the Court was passing on the case due to Repaci's injury. Neither Patrolman McCole nor Sergeant Gallante, Repaci's two colleagues, had been similarly called. It was also significant that three different judges were sitting over that period: Thomas E. Jones, Julius Helfand, and Guy Mangano. Each of them took the trouble to suggest to Lynn (in a whispered conversation in front of the bench) that a trial was really not necessary in this case, that a deal should be worked out.

It was inevitable that Lynn should find this procedure sufficiently harassing that he openly considered the possibility of counter-charging the District Attorney's office with malicious prosecution. In the end he made it clear to the judge, with Assistant DA Greenberg present, that his client had no intention of pleading guilty to anything, that he was innocent of any and all crimes, that the grotesque truth of the matter was that it was the police who were the proper defendants, not Blutcher, having shaken him down repeatedly and beaten him up when he refused to pay. He requested that there be no further summonses to appear until the actual trial date, and that it be set with the knowledge of Repaci's capacity to appear.

It was with high expectancy, then, that the defendant and his attorney received notification that trial would commence on May 5. Lynn took pains to contact Greenberg and was informed that the People were, indeed, finally prepared to go. Lynn, of course, indicated much the same. And once again, he advised Blutcher to alert the witnesses, also suggesting that he invite as many of his friends and family as possible in order to pack the courtroom. It was his belief that their presence might serve as an influence over the court and its conduct of the trial, showing the solidarity of the black community against the oppressions of the police.

Again, Blutcher spent his weekend in just such preparations, taking special pains to visit the Trottas, father and son, and left them, assured that they were willing and able to testify.

Bernard Trotta was the kind of plodding, hard-working man who looked a lot older than he was. Life seemed to mark him more severely than most of his contemporaries: gray hair, wrinkled brow, tired eyes, stoutness of body. He even felt older than his forty-four years. He thought of himself as an easy-going man who got along well with his neighbors and his co-workers. He was a good family man and considered himself fortunate to have such a fine spirited wife. He was a responsible man, having worked for the same company for seventeen years.

It did not surprise him when Larry Blutcher first visited him, early in January, about being prepared to testify at the trial. He was willing to do what he could to help. He would come to the court with his son, Dexter. It was only right that they should do this. After all, everybody around knew how hard Larry had tried to make good in that store, how the police came around for the take, how an ugly incident like that could happen. Trotta had seen and heard enough on that Sunday to be able to help in court. Dexter, too. He had no doubt of that. That first time, he had spent the night preparing himself and his son, remembering exactly what had happened. After all, it had been over a year since the incident. They had to get their stories straight. That Dexter's memory was a lot sharper than his should not have surprised him; everybody knew that kids were that way. But then, sometimes they imagine things, too, going off on little flights of their own, maybe. Bernard Trotta had seen enough cross examinations on TV shows to know what you're likely to come up against. The smart DA wasn't going to just let him and Dexter say anything without questioning it. Over and over, probably. He tried to picture that, wondering if he could be tripped up.

It started to worry him, especially after all the delays. Week after week. What was the matter with the courts? Blutcher would come around and tell him how the trial was about to begin, how he and Dexter must come to testify, maybe on Tuesday, maybe on Wednesday, and Trotta started to get annoyed. Everything seemed so shaky. It seemed to him that they were making it very difficult for Blutcher, hanging him up this way, stalling him week after week. And then he began to think that maybe he didn't like the prospects for himself, either.

He doubted, and he did not bother to question his doubts. It was the way of blacks in the ghetto to fear the cops and courts, to keep clear of them at all times. If ever a black could pinpoint enemy territory, it was the Precinct house and the courtroom. The more touchy the case, the bigger the stakes, and the more likely the trouble. Trotta had been seventeen years on the job, but he was not without need to worry about eighteen. His family was not on welfare, but he was never so sure that there might not come a time when they needed it. And the police . . . did he really think he and his son could testify against the word of the police and not have to pay a price of some kind? And what would happen if they did? What would happen to Dexter?

Nor was Trotta encouraged to testify by his friends. He would see their chary, ambivalent looks when it came up. The trial. Yes, the trial. Everybody had some kind of a story about how they knew somebody who'd testified and gotten zapped in some way. Sure, Trotta knew it wouldn't be that fearsome—in fact, his own wife kept insisting that he go through with it. (She was big with that new black stick-together thing.) But what was there to gain? If only he and his son weren't the *only* ones to testify.

It wasn't long before Larry sensed the man's waning enthusiasm. If Trotta's answer was always an affirmative one, his manner seemed somewhat evasive. He would agree to come with his son, yes, but he didn't seem to be concerned about the exact time or place they would be needed. Were the old instructions that firmly fixed in his mind? Then, too, Larry had heard the usual stories about the penalties for testifying against the police—nor could he deny the alleged threats in the neighborhood since the week of the incident itself, the sudden disappearance of the other witness, Beverly Harris. There was the matter involving the rival grocery across the street from 960 Lafayette, the one owned by the Puerto Rican, Marrero Ponce. One night, not long since, it had been fire-bombed. The whole store had gone up in a blast of fire and smoke and nothing was left of it. Ponce himself had disappeared from the neighborhood. Some said it was because he had refused to give a man credit for a pack of cigarettes. Others said that maybe, just maybe, it had something to do with the police. Was Ponce being shaken down? Had he, too, refused to pay? Had he threatened to testify for Larry? Since nobody knew, all sorts of rumors ran rampant. And what could Larry say to counter them?

He told Conrad Lynn of his fears. He simply did not know any more whether Trotta would show up at the trial.

To Lynn, this was a familiar problem. His advice was to keep working on him, impressing him with the need for his testimony.

And when the day came when he was likely to be called, Larry himself had to be there to pick him up, along with his son, and personally bring him to court.

Couldn't he be subpoenaed? Blutcher asked.

Lynn acknowledged that such an action was not unusual, but in this instance he did not think it wise. Not only did it sometimes fail to get your witnesses there (they call in sick or simply disappear for the day); what was even more damaging, they run scared and become unsympathetic witnesses; they hedge on their testimony, they turn against you. The only real help that the Trottas could give the defense was a willing disposition to testify. The very nature of their statements would not be conclusive anyway.

What it boiled down to, Lynn knew, was whether he could convince a jury that the police were liars. The policeman's lie, that was the enemy. As Paul Chevigny has written: ". . . the lie becomes the chief abuse of authority. The entire legal system founders on this abuse . . . for once an arrest is made, the police need a conviction (to justify it) and lying is simply an accepted part of getting it."

The problem is compounded by the inevitable follow-up: the entire police force will back the policeman's testimony, however great the lie. "Indeed, it is a commonly accepted premise." Chevigny adds, for example, that researchers have learned that 11 out of 15 policemen would not report a brother officer for taking money from a prisoner, and 10 out of 13 said they would not testify against the officer if he were accused by the prisoner. It is all merely part of the normal procedure employed to preserve the policeman's authority and, under circumstances of stress, his job itself. In the ultimate goal of professional solidarity, almost any means are justified.

Lynn was ready to take the gamble. Get the Trottas to court without a subpoena. They could be extremely helpful to counter the policemen's lie. Especially the boy. Lynn had not met young Dexter, but from what he had heard, he was bright and personable, with a friendly, open face. Even his stoutness was an asset. People tend to trust a fat person over a lean one. Hopefully, the jury would be sympathetic. It would be difficult for the prosecution to counter that sympathy with an aggressive cross examination. After all, he was only a twelve-year-old boy . . .

As Lynn put it: "The oldest rule of thumb in the book is 'Never expect anything from a jury.' A jury is as enigmatic and unreliable as a day in April. Sympathetic or hostile, depending on human factors no one is ever able to predict. I would work for a hung jury, right from the beginning. I would try to get two or three Jewish women, apt to be sympathizers, at least not hate-ridden . . . maybe two or three blacks, no more than that: too many blacks makes them overly cautious of their strength and they'd tend to lean over backwards . . . what I don't want is a batch of retired Con Ed clerks who'd spent their lives accepting the Establishment and its authority. The Brooklyn jury lists were full of such people, and they thrive on convicting anyone who isn't a retired Con Ed clerk—especially ghetto blacks in confrontations with cops.

"I plan to attack, right from the beginning. In my opening statement, I wanted to plant in their minds that Patrolman Repaci almost killed the defendant. He attacked out of anger. A black man dared to defy him and he boiled over. I wasn't going to quibble over legalisms. The DA was going to have to prove that Blutcher was some sort of wild and savage type who'd attack two armed cops twice his size . . . well, I'd reverse it: I'd say those two cops actually wanted to kill him!"

So they came to court on Monday morning, May 5, all fired up with the challenge that faced them—only to discover, once again, that this was just one more incidence of stalling. Neither Repaci (who was still in the hospital) nor McCole appeared. There was no intention by the People to open.

If Lynn was angered, he did not so indicate. He would not give Greenberg the satisfaction. He was called to the bench for one more whispered conversation with the latest in the continuous chain of judges and the attempt at effecting a deal.

"It was another deliberate effort by the system to break us down. Those judges have regular weekly meetings in which these cases are discussed with the District Attorney's office. They know exactly what's going on. They have continued to call us back—just as had been done with the Sabbath violation summons—in an attempt to make it impossible for me to continue with this case, hoping that I would convince Blutcher to cop a plea."

In effect, Lynn was sufficiently exercised about the maltreatment of his client that he called the new Brooklyn District Attorney, Eugene Gold, to complain of malicious prosecution, telling him the entire history of the case. Gold was immediately struck by the significance of the indictment number, 2502, for higher numbers had long since been adjudicated. He assured Lynn he would investigate.

Lynn speculated: "The way it seemed, they just didn't want to put this case on trial. Any case involving police brutality, especially in Brooklyn, was a touchy business, and the ingredients of this one, with shakedowns and all, must have seemed threatening. They had been doing all the stalling they could possibly do, and if they had their way, they'd keep right on stalling. At the same time, the approach of summer must have been in the back of their minds. You pass that day in the calendar when it says 'summer' and all the fine folk who run the city begin to get very nervous. A case like this, it could make any politician nervous, and the courts, they're just as much a part of the politics of the city as the Mayor's office. The trouble was, nobody wanted to touch it. The judges included. And you couldn't blame them . . ."

A week later, Eugene Gold himself called Lynn, informing him that Repaci was to be discharged from the hospital, and the trial date had been conclusively set for June 9.

If Blutcher shrugged with well-deserved skepticism, Lynn believed the summons this time. He respected Gold. Besides, he was the District Attorney; having set the date himself, he would have no one to blame if there was another slip-up. As the famous sign on former President Harry Truman's desk put it: THE BUCK STOPS HERE.

On June 9, eighteen months after the incident, the People of the State of New York were finally ready for Laurence Blutcher.

12

The Supreme Court Building is a modern stone structure in the Brooklyn Civic Center, fronting on the historic avenue known as Fulton Street, the original link to the ferry slip less than a mile away that connected Brooklyn with Manhattan. Through the large windows of the courthouse, one can see the distant skyscrapers of New York, while immediately below, over 200 maples stand neatly in long rows, all very much the same size, their lush foliage supplying an appealingly cool green in contrast to the shimmering white heat of sun on concrete. Beyond them, a row of office buildings, each housing at least one bank, their names demanding attention over the tops of the maples: Brooklyn Savings Bank, Kings County Lafayette Trust, Bank of Commerce, Central State Bank, Chemical Bank.

People vs. Blutcher had long since been assigned to Part IX of the Supreme Court, Criminal Term. On June 9, 1969, a few minutes after 10 A.M., the bailiff unlocked the door of Room 741, where its legal business would be conducted, and the few people who were waiting outside took seats along the three rows of long wooden benches to the rear of the court. At the front, the huge plaque that overhung the judge's chair read with majesty: WHERE LAW ENDS, THERE TYRANNY BEGINS: WILLIAM PITT, while below, the familiar high-backed, maroon leather swivel chair awaited the judge who would preside. To the side, the United States flag hung limply on its stand, and the court clerk, a competent old hand with a tired round face and thinning gray hair, fussed with his papers, preparing to organize the day's calendar, occasionally interrupted by attorneys asking for information or requesting favors. By 10:15, over a dozen people had gathered, mostly black criminals and their white lawyers. The initial order of business would include the sentencing of the court for trials recently concluded.

In the rear, a tall, well-dressed man around forty, with horn-rimmed glasses and a thin, neatly trimmed mustache, sat reading the *New York Times*. By his appearance, one might guess him to be an executive for an ad agency or, perhaps, a stockbroker. There was none of the intensity about his manner to suggest he was an attorney. He seemed totally at ease, like a patient, relaxed man in a hotel lobby who had arrived early for an appointment. He was, in fact, a Court Follower. A hobby, as it were. Semi-retired from a successful career in real estate, an occupation he found less than stimulating, he found excitement in the dramatic atmosphere of the courts and spent his leisure time following trials. "Some people go to the movies a lot, or sit in the park and feed the pigeons. I like to come here to see the action. You learn about people, about the way they conduct themselves. You learn about the law and what a farce it is. Oh, I consider myself quite an expert on the law. My youngest son and I, we're New York Jet football fans, and we go to all the games at Shea Stadium, and he considers himself quite an expert at that. It's a passion with him—keeps a scrapbook and studies it. I suppose you might say that this is my passion. It's fascinating. If you're aware of the nuances, you realize how subtle the drama can be . . ."

Larry Blutcher came in with Monica around 10:10, knowing through experience that it would be a long time before his case was called. Conrad Lynn arrived shortly after him, his dark, battered attaché case held tightly in his hand. (There were other times and circumstances when he kept it chained to his wrist. "Any time I was working on a case the FBI was interested in, I knew they'd be following me, and anything they could do to get information was considered fair game, especially my briefcase. Once, at an airport, I merely set the case on the floor while I fished in my pocket for a dime to buy a newspaper; it couldn't have been ten seconds, but that's all they needed. It was gone. Of course, I had only shirts and socks in it; I'd kept my papers in my suitcase. After that, however, I took to chaining it to me.") He sat down beside his client with intent to ask about those witnesses when he felt an interrupting hand on his shoulder. He looked up into the now-familiar, friendly face of the Assistant District Attorney, Sheldon Greenberg.

"Do you have a moment, Mr. Lynn?"

Lynn followed him into the hall, speculating on what new prospects might be in store for him. "I guess I should have known. He was very polite, as always, asked me how I was and all, and then he told me, like before, that he didn't think this case need go to trial. He was worried about all the black-white tensions in Brooklyn. Everybody was. I guess he was especially worried about all the fuss I might try to kick up. I have that reputation, and it follows me around, you know, as in the Westerns, the movies, when a man is known as the fastest gun. Well, I couldn't blame him, but I didn't say anything. Let him think that. I just waited for whatever he had to offer. He said to me that he'd worked it out—presumably with his boss, Eugene Gold —he could get the assault charges reduced all the way down to disorderly conduct. Blutcher could plead guilty to disorderly conduct and absolutely nothing would be put on his criminal record. He would be released, a free man, and the whole business would be over.

"Well, I stood there pretending to think about it. Then I told him I would inform my client of this, but I didn't think he would go for it. He was an innocent man and he insisted on a complete expression of his innocence. He wanted the court to respect that and he was ready to go the whole way toward gaining an acquittal. I reminded Greenberg of our last conversation before a different judge, how I explained that those cops were shaking him down, how it was the cops who should be on trial, not Blutcher, and how Greenberg himself had to agree with me about that. Oh, he didn't like to hear all that. He said he thought it was going to be a mistake for me if we didn't accept this deal. He said he could fix it so we wouldn't win, sounding as if there were no question of it. I replied that we were going to trial anyway. He shook his head sadly and said something about how he didn't want a decent young man like my client having to go to prison for this. I guess he was trying to make me feel responsible for it."

Lynn returned to his client and informed him of this latest ploy. Blutcher immediately shook it off. Not interested. As Lynn had suggested to Greenberg, Larry wanted to go the whole way —regardless of the risk.

It was close to 10:25 when the clerk announced the arrival of the judge. "Hear ye, all interested parties in Part IX, Criminal Court, please rise, Judge Joseph Corso, presiding . . ."

The judge was a short, slight man, well into middle age, his thinning silver hair well-barbered, combed tightly against his scalp. He wore glasses in the way a man does when he has worn them all his life, never fingering them, as if they were part of his face. He nodded politely to the clerk, barely looking at the others assembled before him. Lynn, seated with his client on those rear benches, did not know Corso and could only speculate about the inadequate tidbits of his reputation. ("A tough, hardline, law-and-order man, but not unfair . . . Tendency to be wordy and a bit stuffy . . . Loves the sound of his own advice . . .") Lynn wondered if, in those weekly sessions over scheduling the court calendar, Judge Corso had volunteered to preside over this case or whether it had been forced upon him. Either way, Lynn did not particularly relish the prospects. He recalled an earlier session in February when an old colleague, Judge Tom E. Jones, was presiding. They had been young, struggling black lawyers together, fellow radicals in the political turbulence of the thirties. A man like Jones would have to be sympathetic to Blutcher. Lynn could only regret that fate and the workings of the system had prevented it. Instead of a black judge presiding over a case involving a black defendant with a black lawyer, an Italian would be judging the testimony of an Italian policeman who had initiated the assault. While such ethnic evaluations seemed blatantly raw and oversimplified, Lynn could not readily discard them as being without consequence. If the country were not so full of bigots, there would be no case of People vs. Blutcher in the first place. However, insofar as his evaluation of Judge Corso was concerned; he would have to wait and see.

When it became clear to Larry Blutcher that his case was going to be tried, that this was not going to be just another stall in what had long seemed to be an endless chain, his stomach suddenly reacted to this awesome reality with painful tightening. It had been such a long time in coming, he thought his sensitivities had been dulled, but now the fuse was lit again. Not without panic, he faced the reality of it. He thought of his witnesses, the two Trottas, wondering if he had been persuasive enough, wondering how strong were *their* fears. Would they show up when needed? Would they? He leaned over in his seat to relax his stomach muscles, aware of a throbbing in his head. He told himself he was just nervous, that was all, that he wasn't going to get a stomach ache or a headache. His head had gotten better, much better. He hadn't had a severe headache for weeks now. He hadn't even brought any Darvon with him. He thought now that maybe it would have been wiser if he had.

It was just after 11 when the pool of veniremen was called. The bailiff moved to the rear of the room, escorted in thirty prospective jurors for the selective process instead of the usual forty-eight; there had been poor planning by the staff and the pool had been left in short supply. Lynn, however, was less concerned by the quantity than the quality. At first glance, he saw a preponderance of middle-aged men (retired?) and very few blacks. There were none he could safely categorize as middle-class Jewish housewives, and more than a few who carried the New York *Daily News*. It was not an encouraging beginning.

Barely five minutes after they had filled the first two rows of benches in the rear, they were asked to leave the courtroom and wait in the hall. Judge Corso, as it turned out, had to sentence a recently convicted man, and the jurors were not permitted to witness this lest his action prejudice their feelings about the judge. Blutcher, meanwhile, was fascinated by the sentencing that was about to take place.

The convicted man stood a few feet from him, disheveled, like one who had spent the night in jail. He was a short black man named Albert Peterson, no older than Blutcher. He had killed a man in a fight over a girl, his mistress. However, sitting in the court were his wife and seven children, all dressed up in their Sunday best, like a family going to church, Larry mused. A white lawyer stood beside him, pleading with the judge that the man deserved sympathy, that he had always been hard-working and had never gotten into any serious trouble with the law prior to this tragic incident, that he had had an extremely difficult life, having had his first child at the age of thirteen, and had struggled to keep his head above water ever since, that the presence of his wife and family in court was an indication of their mutual devotion, that, finally, the whole business with the other woman was one of those tragic mistakes that come out of being black in the ghetto.

It was all very academic, of course. (The Court Follower could have set anyone straight about that, knowing that the judge's mind had long since been made up as to sentencing.) As it turned out, Judge Corso had decided to be lenient, or so he interpreted his sentence. He told Peterson that he was sending him away for seven years, largely "because of the impassioned plea of his attorney," that he could have made it far more. . . .

Blutcher saw the man turn and look past him, one final glance at his wife and the kids as they put the handcuffs on him, a soft, sad smile on his face to show how courageous he could be. "Wow, a woman can sure mess up a man. I mean, you see this Peterson take that last look at his wife and you know that man has had his troubles. I thought, how many times did I get in trouble over a woman? Enough. Enough. I felt the goose bumps all over me like when you think how close you'd just come to getting run down by a truck. Peterson, he couldn't become a man. He's just a kid and he makes her pregnant and they make him marry her. Then he grows up but he doesn't have a chance. How could he? I thought of all the women I'd been with, how I used them and loved them in one way or another, but mostly, how I couldn't be any good with them because I wasn't a real man. I was just another poor black slob who didn't know how to live. I mean, you have to have a focus in order to love a woman proper. You can't be a slob on one hand and still be good with a woman on the other. It just ends up bad every time."

The bailiff marched Peterson away and the clerk called another to stand before the judge. "He was black, too. I'd been coming here for over six months now, and I'd seen a lot of people coming in and out of court, and it gets so you think that's the way it is, the DA and judges and juries and lawyers are pretty much all white and the defendants are pretty much all black. Like the cat they had up there now, young, they're always young, too, and he'd been accused of trying to steal a radio from a store, but he didn't really steal it because a cop had caught him before he could actually take it, and the jury had said he was not guilty. He stood before the judge, real stiff and silent, and Judge Corso, he actually told this cat that he thought the jury was stupid. He said that jury was the stupidest damn jury he had ever presided over, and that they had let him off when they should have found him guilty. The judge got real angry. He told him he *knew* he was guilty, but the law said he had to let him go even though he was ready to bet that he'd see him again for some other crime, he'd see him again, and the next time he wouldn't be so lucky and the judge was going to throw the book at him.

"I thought, wow, from where I was sitting, I was stuck with the wrong judge and too late for the right jury."

At 11:30, the thirty prospective jurors returned, and the court made ready for the impaneling. Arbitrarily, the clerk moved the first dozen into the jury box and announced that the court permitted five peremptory challenges—wherein an attorney could dismiss any five jurors he simply did not want to sit, and his reasons would go unchallenged—and unlimited challenges for cause —wherein an attorney must convince the court that a prospective juror was not fit to serve. He then turned the jury over to the prosecution.

"How do you do, ladies and gentlemen. My name is Sheldon Greenberg, I'm the Assistant District Attorney who will prosecute this case . . ."

He smiled graciously as he spoke his greeting, his manner intimate and warm, like a man introducing himself at a cocktail party. It was clear, however, that he was aware of his serious purpose, and his charm was not a sign of levity but a mark of his maturity. He maneuvered his bulky frame with caution, careful not to appear clumsy lest anyone think contemptuously of him. If he was less than graceful or athletic, he was very much in control, his large round head projecting formidably from sagging shoulders, his young jowly face and squinty eyes more friendly and earnest than intimidating. Then, too, he was young, younger than anyone else attached to the case, including the defendant. It was his size and weight that made him appear older, to which he added an intensity of manner that lent gravity to his function.

Born thirty-two years before in the Bronx, he was 100 per cent New York City—every gesture, every inflection so indicated. He had gone through Stuyvesant High School, then Pittsburgh University, and got his law degree after attending law school at Brooklyn. In 1961, one year later, he joined the District Attorney's office at a salary of $5500, the first such staff member under 30, and for three-and-a-half years, he learned his trade from the bottom up, ferreting around police stations to investigate police confessions and substantiate evidence. He then worked at the Indictment Bureau, presenting hundreds of cases to the Grand Jury, learning the intricate details and nuances of the law so that the evidence would stand up in court. "It was an invaluable experience for me." Several years before, he had been promoted to his current job, at $12,000 a year, where he had tried over sixty cases, although "nothing of great consequence." He lived in the East Flatbush area of Brooklyn with his wife and two young children. He could face the twelve prospective jurors like a man who belonged there.

"The people of this city have pointed a finger at Mr. Laurence Blutcher," he told them, pointing his own finger across the room at the defendant. His huge body stiffened as he said this, his tone lending tremendous importance to all their presence. "The Grand Jury has heard the facts and handed down an indictment against him. Now, is there any one of you who believe you cannot be fair and impartial, for any reason whatsoever, in evaluating the evidence as it shall be presented?"

He paused, allowing a moment of instant decision, and three jurors rose to excuse themselves, one of whom was a black woman. Greenberg stood quietly by as the clerk immediately replaced them.

"Is there anyone here with any members of his family or close friend in law enforcement?" he continued, and when three others nodded, yes, they had close friends who were police officers, Greenberg explained that it would be up to him, the prosecutor, to prove the facts, the defense need do nothing, absolutely nothing, for that is the essence of American justice. Could all of them be absolutely fair in interpreting the facts?

When he began his examination of each juror in turn, it became immediately clear that this would be more than a test of their fitness, but his own attempt to charm them all. "Would you, sir, as a man with an executive position in your professional life, would you be able to reason with others of menial backgrounds? You know, you can't simply make up your mind, then go to the men's room and wait until the other eleven decide to agree with you . . ." Yes, the others laughed as the juror smiled in agreement. "And you, madam, you say your sister has been the victim of assault and robbery in the streets . . . would you be fair and impartial in the case of this young man, to hear the evidence as presented and not prejudge him in any way?" See? He is not just looking out for himself, he is actually protecting the defense! "And, you, madam, would you please speak up just a bit so Mr. Lynn over there across the room can hear you." Then he digs for any prejudice against policemen, just to show he is a man who knows his side of the case, too. "Have you had any bad experiences with police officers, sir? Anything that might make it difficult for you to evaluate the testimony of a policeman? Were you driving along the Belt Parkway, for example, at barely thirty-five miles an hour, when you heard that awful siren?" That, too, amuses them all, especially the juror he is questioning, and Greenberg smiles with them, enjoying his own joke. "Me, I haven't gotten a single ticket since I've worked in the District Attorney's office . . ." More laughter, at which he feigns indignation. "Well, I've been driving more carefully . . ." and everyone laughs again. He jests, but it is the jesting of a somber man, designed to lighten the burdens of his duties. Again, his humor adds to the gravity of his style.

He spoke with each of them, learning their professions and something of their attitudes, constantly adding, bit by bit, to their knowledge of the case about to be put before them. When he confronted the one black before him, a middle-aged postal employee, he made no mention of race or any of the racial tensions at the root of the whole matter, but bemused the juror by turning this aspect of the case upside down: "Will you, sir, hold me to my duty to prove my case beyond a reasonable doubt . . . ?" as if the black man were, indeed, much too inclined to be on the DA's side and not the black defendant's. It was altogether a disarming exhibition, deftly designed to show his humanity, dispelling any possible notion that he, as a DA, was in the TV image of a bloodthirsty prosecutor seeking to hang some helpless defendant. Indeed, all he sought was fairness for both sides, more like a referee than a contestant. He was, in fact, so humble and sugary that once, when interrupted by the court over a problem of rescheduling, he returned to the jury with an effusive apology, to which the judge himself took exception: "Mr. Greenberg, you really don't have to apologize to the jury. After all, I ordered you to stop." His probing moved swiftly through fifteen minutes, just long enough to establish his competence and his warmth, and when he turned the jury over to Conrad Lynn, one got the feeling that he left them feeling very pleased with both themselves and with him.

Lynn walked slowly toward the jury, slight, wiry, and intense, where Greenberg was soft and ingratiating. Lynn was a gray-bearded black radical with a courtroom style that had been cultivated through years of flamboyant in-fighting against hostile forces far more powerful than himself and his generally highly unpopular clients. Like any experienced attorney, he knew the importance of this introductory confrontation with the jury. He could not play Greenberg's two-headed game. Indeed, he could only wonder how long Greenberg himself would continue to play it. At the same time, he could not antagonize them with any indications of his indignation. "I agree with the District Attorney," he began. "This is what we are looking for: justice." His voice was soft and gentle, a kindly father talking to his troubled son, and the crowded room became hushed as though more weighty words were about to be spoken. He stood close to the jurors, his hand resting on the wooden barrier in front of the jury box, and his eyes rested on the back of his hand as he spoke like one who found knowledge in its wrinkles. "There are no scientific devices to determine guilt or innocence. It must be through you jurors and your thinking on what you hear in court. There will be police officers testifying on one side and private individuals on the other. You have to be careful in your evaluation. Has this private citizen received an impartial treatment?" He looked up at them now, taking a moment to show with his eyes that he was, indeed, a deeply troubled man. "It is not so easy these days, there is so much turmoil. Police power . . . law and order. TV shows of violence and controversy . . . newspaper stories of crime and disorder . . . We are all affected by this. It all gets down to a question of your honesty and your probing for the truth. I must ask of you: are there any feelings that you might be sensitive to, to color your evaluations? Can you really be impartial?"

The question was rhetorical, but several jurors nodded. Lynn smiled at them, having finished his introductory remarks, then moved down the bench toward juror number one. "Mr. Caleano . . ." he read the name from the jury chart in front of him. "You said before that you have a nephew who has recently become a police officer. Suppose you were asked here to consider that a policeman had violated the law. Could you be fair about a consideration of that?"

The DA, however, was not about to leave him a completely open door. His voice rang through the hushed courtroom like the sudden snap of a whip. "Objection! There is no such thing in the indictment!"

It was the first bit of controversy, an indication of hostilities to come. The judge smiled, though startled at the outburst, then weighed the issue as he tapped his pencil against his pad. "I think we can allow that, Mr. Greenberg," he said.

To another with an Italian-sounding name, Lynn pressed further in emphasizing what he sought to interpret as the essence of the case: "I assume, sir, that you have no special national feelings that will make you partial? No racial feelings . . . ?" And then, to a woman who might be sensitive to blacks as potential muggers: "Do you have any special feelings about colored people that might affect your judgment in this case?" To the black postal worker: "Do you feel you might be prejudiced toward policemen as fellow government employees?" Throughout his probing, he kept asking which of them had been victims of any crimes, what kind—auto thefts? muggings?—and which of them had social relations with law-enforcement people. Where Greenberg had sought to pacify the jury by the de-emphasizing controversy, Lynn kept carping at it—race, cops, violence, prejudice—challenging them all to take cognizance of the black-white tensions of the times.

("I did not want to pretend this was merely a case about a young man and two police officers. It was a case about a young black man and two white police officers, and everyone had better be direct about it. If anyone on that jury was prejudiced—and one could bet at least some of them were—they were going to be just as prejudiced if I'd said nothing at all. At least this way, I put them on the defensive . . .")

In the end, both Lynn and Greenberg used three peremptory challenges. Significantly, the defense chose to remove the executive, a retired clerk, and the man who had once been mugged (he was also a reader of the *Daily News*). To the replacements, Greenberg once again admonished that they be fair, reminding them that the defendant was innocent until proven guilty. And to the two alternates, he gave the advice: "You are like a pinch hitter in a baseball game. You must be ready, alert, pay attention . . ."

Through the several hours involved in this process, Larry Blutcher sat quietly and stoically, alternately fascinated by the process and depressed by the results. "Mr. Lynn, he asked me a few times, was there anyone I didn't like, anyone I didn't want to sit on the jury? The way I saw it, there was hardly one I *did* want. I mean, only one black man. That was all. There was a black lady, but she backed out as fast as you could say Jim Crow. Excused herself at the first chance. I was glad to see her go, all right. She looked like she was scared to death already. I looked at the others but they hardly glanced at me. I saw the black postal man looking once, but even he looked away real quick. I told that to Mr. Lynn and he laughed. He said, Who did I think I was, Diahann Carroll?"

Judge Joseph Corso glanced at his notes and then began, explaining to the jury the structure of the trial to follow. "The District Attorney will open the case, outlining the general nature of the proof he has prepared to substantiate the indictment. He will explain the message of his witnesses. What he says, however, is not evidence. Only the witnesses can produce evidence . . ." He spoke slowly and clearly, making sure every point was understood, the diligent teacher before an unfamiliar and insecure group of students. "Next, the defense attorney, Mr. Lynn, *may* outline his defense. He doesn't have to. The defendant is always presumed to be innocent before this court. It is up to the District Attorney to prove him guilty . . ." It was the essence of this man that he fully believed in the American system of justice and the effectiveness of the courts in maintaining that justice.

Joseph R. Corso had been born in Brooklyn, sixty-one years before. As he put it: "I was born, bred, and buttered in Brooklyn." His father, a Singer Sewing Machine salesman in Italy, had come to America in 1898 and continued in the same line of work. The son went through Bushwick High School and studied law at Fordham University Law School. He was admitted to the bar at the age of twenty-four, spent the next seventeen years in a general law practice. Then elected to the New York State Legislature, he spent another seventeen years as a Democrat in Albany. Recently, he had been elected Judge in the Civil Court, then resigned to run for the Supreme Court where he now sits.

"The District Attorney will then call his witnesses. You must watch closely and listen carefully. Do you believe them? Do you think they are telling the truth? Or, perhaps, they are hedging on the truth. It will be up to you to decide . . ."

The judge was a hard worker. He arrived early every morning, then sat in his chambers and reviewed the notes he took some-times late into the preceding night. He was like an eager young man trying to make good in a new profession.

"Mr. Lynn may then do the same for the defense. He may do absolutely nothing. Remember, it is not necessary for the defense to say a word. It is up to the DA to convince you that the defendant is guilty of the charges beyond a reasonable doubt . . ."

He still lived in Brooklyn, along Bushwick Avenue in what was left of the upper-middle-income area. He had seen the erosion of neighborhoods in the passage of time. He remembered Mayor Hylan of New York, who once lived in a mansion in his area. "It is now a dilapidated shack." Yes, and around the corner, the beginning of the ever-expanding Brooklyn jungle. "It is all very different now. Everyone my age who is still here has stories to tell. It is a sad thing to see. One of the saddest things of all was the departure of the Brooklyn Dodgers. I used to be quite a baseball fan. I think we all were, one way or another. When the Dodgers left, a big piece of what was Brooklyn went with them. And I stopped being a baseball fan." He lives pleasantly and comfortably. One of his daughters is married, a schoolteacher; the other works at the N.Y.U. Medical Center. He has a summer home at Mattituck, a small beach-side town on eastern Long Island's north shore, where he spends sunny weekends like the one that had just ended.

"When I sustain an objection, whatever the witness says must be stricken from your minds as well as from the court record . . . A question itself does not constitute evidence, only the answer does . . . Take the law from me as I give it to you whether you like it or not. I want you to know, I do not have time to form an opinion as to the defendant's innocence or guilt: that is up to you."

After having heard these three gentlemen of the legal profession, a juror might well have come to the opinion that he was about to sit in judgment at the trial of the century. In the end, the judge would tell them all that they were, in fact, participating in one of the greatest functions of American democracy: to be jurors at a criminal trial. For this was the best system of justice conceived by the most brilliant minds in civilized history—a trial of a defendant by a jury of his peers.

Blutcher exulted in all this explanatory detail. At the same time, he knew more than enough to be sceptical. Somewhere in all those grandiose words there was a hole . . .

"Well, let's hope the system works," he said quietly to Conrad Lynn.

Lynn smiled and shook his head. "It always works, Larry; the question is, for whom?"

13

"I give you the bone structure of the case. The evidence is the meat . . ." Assistant DA Sheldon Greenberg was telling the jury in his opening statement. "In order for you to put the meat on the bones, you've got to know what the structure will be. Well, it all began a long time ago. December 3, 1967. The defendant, Mr. Laurence Blutcher, was operating a grocery store at 960 Lafayette Avenue, Brooklyn. A Sunday. The law says that you're not supposed to be open for business on Sunday . . ."

(Well, there it was, Lynn speculated: the opening wedge offered on a silver platter, as it were. The false interpretation of the Sabbath Law. So quick, so easy, so foolish. It was such an obvious blunder, Lynn began to wonder: was this, perhaps, a tactic? Or could it possibly be that Greenberg simply did *not* know the details of the Sabbath Law?)

". . . Two patrolmen, McCole and Repaci, were on duty that day, in a squad car. They saw the lights on in Blutcher's store, but when they tried the door, it was locked. They told the defendant that if he opened the store, they would have to give him a summons for violating the Sabbath Law, and then they left. A few hours later, they returned, and they saw that the store was, indeed, open. So McCole went in to write him a summons. 'What is your name?' Laurence Blutcher would not identify himself. An argument started, so they called the sergeant, who arrived a few minutes later, the mediator. 'He won't identify himself,' McCole told him. 'Identify yourself,' the sergeant commands. The argument flares up again, and at one point it stops being an argument and becomes a fight. And how does that happen? That happens when the defendant picks up a weapon. Not a gun. Not a knife. Not a cannon, an ax, or a hand grenade. It's a grocery store, so he picked up a jar of pickles and he flung it at Patrolman Repaci, and it struck him on his left hand and it broke his thumb, and then it hit him in the chest and fell to the floor and smashed. Repaci then said: 'Now, you're under arrest,' but when he went to take Laurence Blutcher into custody, Laurence Blutcher didn't want to be taken into custody. He felt he was within his rights to break the officer's thumb and he resisted arrest. A fight started, and Blutcher was getting the best of Patrolman Repaci, so Repaci had to take out his gun and turn it around—because he wasn't going to shoot Blutcher over a jar of pickles and a Sabbath violation—and he defended himself with his gun, and he hit Blutcher over the head. And he may have caused Blutcher some injury . . ."

("*Some* injury . . . ?" Lynn made his second note. Did Greenberg really believe he could get away with such a distortion?)

"Senseless? Maybe, had cooler heads prevailed, nothing would have happened. I don't know. That's not for us to decide. What you must decide is, what about the indictment? The indictment charges assault in the second degree. Assault. It says that Laurence Blutcher had a certain intent, it was to stop Patrolman Repaci from performing his lawful duty: and with that intent, he did an act; he assaulted an officer and caused physical injury to that officer. The indictment also alleges that he resisted the arrest, and he did this through an assault . . .

"When all of the evidence is in, you will make your determination whether, from that witness stand, you heard evidence that shows you beyond a reasonable doubt that Laurence Blutcher had the intent I described, that he struck the officer with this intent. You will make this decision without passion, without prejudice either way. You'll make it justly and intelligently upon the evidence, because if you base it on anything other than the evidence, it's not a just verdict. . . ."

(Lynn bristled at this hypocrisy. Greenberg was obviously talented at playing both sides. Let no one say he has even a smidgen of prejudice. Let the world know he is not a bigot. There's the black man, the defendant, and shortly, there will be the white cops . . . but you must not be prejudiced, dear jurors. You must convict the black man on what the white cops tell you because that's the meat of my case. Yes, Greenberg was a clever fellow.)

"I'm not here to shriek for the blood of the defendant. I'm not here to bring the rafters down and say you must convict this man. It's not the way we do things. If you calmly go over the evidence you are about to hear and decide on the guilt or innocence of the defendant upon that evidence, your verdict must bespeak truth and bring justice. We ask no more. Thank you . . ."

It was time for the defense to speak—if it wished. If Lynn ever had any doubts as to whether he ought to, they were dispelled by Greenberg's sweet distortions.

He approached the jury shaking his head sadly, like one who sometimes finds the problems of life too burdensome. There was, however, no plaintiveness in his tone. He was merely very much in earnest. He would jar this jury, yes, but not with any histrionics.

"I think you can understand why it is that we were so careful earlier in the day that nothing would impede your judgment . . . because there is unquestionably a very sharp dispute on

what occurred on December 3, in every particular . . ." He
paused for a moment, like a marksman making sure his aim was
accurate, then fired point-blank: "The prosecution is construct-
ing a case which has no validity whatsoever!" The jury did not
bat an eye, but he knew it must have sunk in. He was tempted to
raise his voice now, but resisted. His passion would be revealed
in what he said, not in the manner he said it. "In the first place,
on December 3, 1967, the police officers, they knew the name of
the defendant. They had seen him on other occasions. They had
been in his store. They knew him. They didn't have to request
his name. Secondly, it's not true that a grocery store may not be
open on Sunday. That's simply not true. A grocery store may be
open on Sunday, so just the fact that the store is open is not the
basis for a policeman, on that alone, coming in to issue a summons . . ." There it was: the whole incident was based on a false
premise—the policemen who allegedly came in to issue a summons for the violation of a law they did not understand. He
stood there in front of the jury and let them ponder that for a
moment. "You are thinking, living, experienced, human beings,
you're going to decide whether this man, admittedly unarmed
with any weapon in the ordinary sense, would, where there were
three policemen, take a jar and out of the blue throw it at a policeman. And these policemen were fully armed. If the man is
sane, it's for you to decide would any man, a grocery-store owner
running a little grocery business, is he going to grab such a bottle and throw it at an officer with intent to do him grievous
harm? It's for you to decide if that story is credible or not."

Lynn looked at them all, a weariness in his eyes that suggested
disbelief that such a thing could be possible. When he spoke
again, his voice rose just enough to indicate his indignation. "Or
will you listen to the defendant and his witnesses' account of how
the police officers knew him in the first place, of what kind of
payoff he had to make, and why it was not that he 'may have
been hurt a little bit' but why he had suffered multiple fractures
of the skull that day and hung between life and death for weeks

in the hospital? Was it because the officers were trying to destroy the evidence of what they had been doing to this man over the months . . . ?"

Larry felt the back of his neck tingling with excitement. These words lifted him right out of himself; he felt like laughing out loud, and he had to gnash his teeth to prevent any embarrassing outburst. "It was like I wasn't here and it was all in the movies or something, and there were all these people, the judge, the jury, and all, and Mr. Lynn was telling them the way it was and they were listening. That's what sent me: they were listening!"

When Lynn sat down, he could not help but wonder if he had made any dent in all those stone faces. Should he have gone over it again, hitting the high points, a capsule version just to cement the issues? Shouldn't he have emphasized the high quality of the defendant's character, to give the jury a greater sense of his responsibility as a store owner? He had been brief as he knew he should be. He had been challenging as he had wished to be. What annoyed him was what always seemed to annoy him: the jury. The twelve impenetrable faces. Somber, always somber, and posed with that sanctimonious look as if being a juror gave them certain holy prerogatives. It was always that way. You could put a dozen Mississippi rednecks in shirts and ties and decent suits, and they would seem just like these people in a jury box. Always the great mystery: what were they thinking? The trouble was, you could be an attorney for a thousand years and you learned nothing about juries except that there was nothing you *could* learn about them. All you could do was pretend that you had them in your camp, charging them with the power of your righteous cause, propelling that charge with a colossal ego that would not acknowledge even the prospect of defeat . . .

It was not an easy job for a black man.

He sat there, his elbow resting on the *New York Times* of that morning. He had hastily fingered through it on the subway, remembering now the quick reference to the celebrated Algiers Motel trial in Michigan where the jury was deliberating, presumably at that very moment, the fate of a Detroit policeman named Ronald August, who had shot and killed a nineteen-year-old black youth. There were no real similarities with this case, certainly not in terms of specifics, yet Lynn could not help but sense that both cases might well turn on the prejudices of the jury and the related emotions of our times. In Michigan, there were twelve whites in the box. In this room, there were 11. If, as it is said, the United States Supreme Court follows the election returns, it is the citizen-juror who creates them. It had been years since Lynn had found gratification in the election returns.

The action began with Patrolman Daniel McCole, Shield #24599, called as first witness by the People of New York, duly sworn by the clerk of the court, his right hand raised high above the old black Bible. Six years a member of the New York City Police Department, assigned to the 79th Precinct from July 14, 1964, to a date less than three weeks prior to the opening of trial.

McCole was a good-looking man in his late twenties. Lean, blond, slightly freckled, he moved like an athlete on his day off, slightly crouched as he walked, even as he sat, his head thrust forward, his eye firmly fixed on whoever he was talking with. He neither smiled nor frowned, his manner perfectly cool and correct, as though all this were just another aspect of being a cop, another part of his job. One would assume he had testified dozens of times before . . .

In response to Greenberg's questions, he detailed his account of the fateful day. Yes, he remembered it all, and from the positive way he spoke, it was as if it had all happened a week before. He was on radio patrol duty with Patrolman Philip Repaci from 7:30 A.M. to 3:30 P.M., the first half as operator, the second as recorder. He patrolled two sectors, Charles and David (C and D); the former included the address of 960 Lafayette Avenue which he approached around 11 A.M. "I observed the gates partially open with the defendant inside the store . . . I knocked on the window and he came to the door, unlocked it, and I informed him that if he opened the store he'll receive a summons. He then said that if I knew what was good for me I wouldn't bother him —something to that effect. I then went back to radio patrol. We came back, it was around 1:25, I observed people inside the store and people coming out with packages. I entered the store and asked the defendant to identify himself, I was going to issue him a summons. There were two people in the store, a male and a young boy. The defendant, he told me if I knew what was good for me, I'd get the—"

McCole paused here, on the brink of an embarrassed smile. After all, he was in a court of law and there were ladies present. "Shall I use his expressions?" he asked Greenberg.

Greenberg nodded. "Yes, please."

"—I'd get the fuck out of his store. He said, 'No motherfucker is going to tell me what to do, get out of my store, these are the white man's laws!'"

Lynn could not but admire the controlled power of McCole's style. But it was this last comment that hit the hardest blow of all. The defendant, McCole was saying, was not merely profane and defiant and criminal, he was also a black-militant rebel, absolutely the most dangerous thing any defendant could be. The black man who defied the white policeman was incriminating himself enough. But the black man who openly defied the white man's law was something else again. Lynn wondered who had set that line so artfully in place. Was that what Greenberg meant when he said he could 'fix it so Blutcher didn't have a chance'?

McCole, meanwhile, was moving full speed ahead:

"Then Repaci entered the store, advised him of the same thing, to identify himself, and the defendant repeated himself to him. I then told Officer Repaci to get the sergeant. Ten minutes later, the sergeant entered the store, told him he could plead not guilty on the summons if he wanted and appear in court. He told the sergeant to go fuck himself. He then proceeded to make a phone call. I don't know who he spoke to, but he was in the phone booth two or three minutes. When he came out, we told him again that if he didn't identify himself he'd be placed under arrest. He then verbally abused us again. We told him, you're under arrest, I then attempted to take him into custody. He threw a punch at myself and pushed Officer Repaci . . ."

To Larry Blutcher, the touch of ecstasy he had felt a few moments before now turned to horror. He sat there sweating as he heard this, bewildered by this violation of his integrity. How could McCole say these things, and in a voice so firm and forceful, like there wasn't a shade of doubt and that this was the truth, the whole truth, and nothing but . . . ? This was McCole, the officer who had stopped Repaci from killing him, McCole who had cried out to Repaci, "Stop. That's enough!" Blutcher wanted to stand up and interrupt the testimony, to shout 'He's lying, he's lying!' but he just sat there, feeling the sweat all over him, saying nothing, shaking a little, holding himself in control. It was as if he had been through this sort of thing already. He felt like a seasoned man-on-trial and that amazed him.

"The defendant then ran back to the counter, picked up a large jar of pickles, hurled it at Officer Repaci, struck him in the hand. He then ran back of the counter. He said: 'No mother-fucker is going to take me out of the store.' He was throwing punches at Repaci and kicks in the back of the counter. The counter was narrow. I couldn't get next to him. Officer Repaci was losing at the time, so he took his gun out, and hit him on the head. He was still struggling, kicking. I reached out to draw him from the counter, but we slipped on the pickles and glass, we were stepping in the juice with our shoes, and we fell. Finally, we put the handcuffs on and dragged him out the door."

Having put this much meat on the bones, Greenberg finished his direct questioning by adding a touch of seasoning. He asked McCole: At any time in the course of your two visits to the premises did you ask the defendant for any money? Did you offer to let him stay open on the Sabbath if he would pay you money? McCole was quick to deny this in a manner that suggested its ludicrousness, and Greenberg turned the witness over to Mr. Lynn for cross-examination.

Conrad Lynn rose slowly, just as slowly approached the witness stand, needing the time to organize his thoughts. It was not going to be easy, he saw that all too clearly. He had only the vaguest notion of an approach to his cross-examination. McCole's testimony was all so cut and dried, so simple, how could he punch holes in it? The way he delivered it made perfect sense. The big lie was buried in the *why* of it all: namely, the shakedown and the defendant's refusal to submit to it. Could he create a doubt about that?

Lynn went to work on McCole as slowly as he could. It was not an unfamiliar technique, frequently likened to a fighter, very light on his feet, circling his opponent, faking with a jab, cocking his right but never throwing it, weaving in and out.

LYNN: Now, do you recall your tour of duty on Sundays as far back as March 1967?

McCOLE: I do not.

LYNN: Now, prior to December 3, can you tell us how long you were patrolling Sector Charles?

McCOLE: That was not normally my sector. I have sector David, but at this time we were short men and we took two sectors.

LYNN: So that was the first day you were in Sector Charles?

McCOLE: No, I've rode in Sector Charles many times.

LYNN: Oh? And prior to December 3, 1967, could you tell the jury when was the prior time you were in Sector Charles?

McCOLE: I could not. I have to look at my memo book.

LYNN: Now, is it possible that three or four weeks before then you had been patrolling Sector Charles?

McCOLE: I don't know at this time.

LYNN: Well, I ask you, isn't it a fact that three or four weeks before December 3, 1967, while you were on duty, you entered the store of Larry Blutcher, the defendant?

McCole: That's false.

Lynn: Even though you're not looking at your memo book?

McCole: I'm positive I'd never been inside that store.

It was clear that the defense could get nowhere on this tack. He tried to challenge McCole on his relationship with the grocery store directly across the street from 960 Lafayette, the store owned by Marrero Ponce, the store that had recently been firebombed. Had McCole observed it on that Sunday? No, he had not, it seemed; he didn't even remember the store at all. Lynn appeared shocked by this; didn't McCole know there was another grocery store across the street? McCole reacted with typical coolness. He had no reason to, he explained: the store was not within the boundaries of the 79th Precinct.

Lynn had swung hard and missed. He shifted his position along the jury box and went back to the attack. He needed a victory now, however small. He reached into his bag and pulled out the plum he had been saving for just such a moment.

Lynn: Now, officer, on that day, you were, among other things, enforcing the law about stores and their observance of the Sabbath?

McCole: That's correct, sir.

Lynn: And were you familiar with the law about stores operating on Sundays?

McCole: I am, sir.

Lynn: What law is that?

Greenberg, however, was not going to let him get away with it and rose to his feet, his voice suddenly louder than the court had yet heard it. "Objection!"

Even before he could explain the nature of his protest, the judge sustained it. Lynn immediately rephrased the question, intent on showing the jury that McCole had no knowledge of the Sabbath Law and its amendments, and that he had no right to be in the defendant's store in the first place.

Lynn: Well, if I were to tell you that the law does, under circumstances—

Again, Greenberg stopped him. "I'm going to object to any statement of law coming from counsel . . ."

Lynn was badgered but undeterred.

LYNN: Now, McCole, when you first went by this store on the morning of December 3, and you saw him opening the store, you, to your mind, that was a violation of what he was permitted to do that day, is that correct?

McCOLE: Upon information from my brother officer, it was.

Then, a few minutes later:

LYNN: You didn't tell him [Blutcher] about why you felt that he shouldn't keep the store open?

McCOLE: I told him he'd be in violation of law.

And still later:

LYNN: And when you first spoke to him as he was standing behind the counter, what did you say to him?

McCOLE: I informed him that he was breaking the Sabbath Law, and I asked him for some identification.

For the moment, this was enough for Lynn. Neither the District Attorney in his opening remarks, nor McCole in his testimony, had indicated that the defendant had, in any way, violated the Sabbath Law. He would use that when the time came.

However, McCole had proved to be as formidable a witness on cross-examination as he had been on direct with the prosecution. Lynn had not been able to shake him. For the benefit of the jury, then, he asked what was less a question than a trial lawyer's statement of position, an emotional declaration to suggest that the witness was, in fact, a liar.

LYNN: Now, isn't it a fact, Officer McCole, that you and Officer Repaci and Sergeant Gallante, all three of you, grabbed the defendant in front of the counter? Isn't that the fact?

McCOLE: No, sir.

LYNN: Isn't it a fact that before you dragged him out of the store, he was already unconscious, in a pool of blood?

McCOLE (bored, like one accustomed to this sort of questioning): No, sir.

At this point, the judge interceded. More merciful than hostile to Lynn, he used the lateness of the hour as an excuse to break —unless Mr. Lynn had something specific he wanted to finish with this line of questioning. No, Lynn replied quite candidly; he was glad for the interruption.

The court was recessed until ten o'clock Tuesday morning.

"Tomorrow afternoon," Lynn told Blutcher as he collected his notes at the table. "Be sure to get those witnesses here for tomorrow afternoon."

The Court Follower stood in the hall as the defense filed out, and he watched them milling around just a few feet from the policemen, saying nothing to each other, each pretending the others weren't there. The drama amused him.

"You hear a policeman testify, they can say pretty much of anything they want and no one puts a finger on them. They act like it was a holiday for them to appear in court, and I suppose that maybe it is. Better than riding patrol all day. A year and a half later, it doesn't matter how long, they remember it all. You take a policeman, he can't remember his mother' name, he can always tell a court exactly what happened a year and a half ago. Lynn, he ought to know it doesn't pay to cross-examine a cop. They give you that earnest look and say whatever they want. They're so sure of themselves, you never know when they're telling the truth. The way I see it, the best thing for Lynn to do is to ignore them. Just ignore them. Let the jury know, he's so contemptuous of them he wouldn't even bother to speak to them. Otherwise, a cop will keep repeating his story over and over, you get so you start believing him. You can't help it. No doubt, he gets so he believes it himself."

Larry Blutcher did not know what to make of it all. He stood in the hall outside the courtroom with Monica and Conrad Lynn, who had a final few words before departing, all very reassuring now. Not ten feet away, there was McCole, and, leaning heavily on crutches, much thinner than before, stood Repaci. It was odd, Larry thought: he did not hate them. They were cops, he realized, and maybe because of that they sometimes acted like the way they had. They just didn't know any different. He could almost get himself to feel sorry for them.

"It was the way you have to think about these things—that it was all part of the whole of things. I could understand that now. The cops do their thing, that's all. They don't understand anything else. It's as natural to them as when a junkie has to steal to supply his habit. It's the system that's wrong, and that's what makes them do what they do. I could look at Repaci and I didn't hate him. He was going to take the stand and tell the same lies that McCole did, but I didn't hate him. Not any more. I walked by him and we looked at each other and he looked away, pretending he didn't even know me. I liked that. I liked the way I felt when I went by him. I felt I was going to win the case, and when I did, it was Repaci who would be the guilty one, not me. It would be the judgment of the court, the white man's court, that said I was innocent, and he would have to live with that on his conscience. It would be my pleasure, then, to say good-bye to him. Good-bye, Officer Repaci. You shook me down, you bugged me in my store, beat me up, arrested me, then you lied in court. It was all part of your white man's system, but you lost in the end. The jury said you were wrong and I was innocent, that you lied and I told the truth. That's what I am going to show everyone."

Larry was aware that there was a basic contradiction in his position, that his faith in the outcome of the trial did not square with his understanding of the hostile system that had brought him here. Had he been challenged then, he would not have argued the point. It was his need for justice that dominated his prognosis. He had to believe that even white man's justice would grant him that. He was thirty-two years old and he had been weaned on a faith in such fundamentals, that truth and innocence would, in the end, be rewarded, that there was an essential goodness in all men. It was, as he now put it, "the will of Allah."

179

"I went home with Monica and we had a drink, and for a while, we didn't talk about the trial at all. Then my mother called, and she wanted to know what happened, and that started it off. I told her that it went very well. I tried to make her feel good about it, I guess. She said she would be there tomorrow. She would be there with the family. She said she was glad that I was feeling so good about it.

"It was true, though. My morale was very much together. Even though 99 per cent of the jury was white, I thought I would win. Monica and me, we talked about it. Sure, the DA was pretty sly and quick, using all that tricknology on the jury. Still, I couldn't see how they would believe him. Me, a single black man, attacking three big white cops armed with .38s by throwing a pickle jar . . ."

He walked with Monica the few blocks to Reid Avenue where the Trottas lived, stopping just long enough to remind Bernard Trotta how much he was needed on the following afternoon. Both he and his son. It was vital to the defense. Trotta said, yes, he would be there, and Larry left with the satisfaction of knowing that, as a result, all would certainly go well.

14

Early on Tuesday morning, Conrad Lynn heard the news while driving into the city: the jury in the Algiers Motel trial in Mason, Michigan, had acquitted the policeman. Three white policemen had killed three black youths, and the first of them was now free. Twelve white jurymen had so determined. Thus, one might say, went the election returns. Lynn knew he would be facing this jury with a different perspective, now. It was inescapable. It didn't matter if none of them had heard the news, they were all subject to the same trends. Like the very atmosphere itself, it sprayed us all with the same pollution; one did not have to read about smog to have smarting eyes.

(The report from Mason, Michigan, stated that Patrolman Ronald August and his family left the courtroom after the acquittal and stepped into a waiting car, where he was asked what he planned to do now. "I'm going to pray," he said.)

When Lynn faced McCole once again, he could not help but read into the cool, red-freckled face a little more defiance, a little more contempt than the previous day. McCole was not on trial and he knew it. Still, it was all part of the same battle, Lynn vs. McCole, wasn't it, and McCole was going to fight that battle because that, too, was part of his job.

LYNN: Patrolman McCole, yesterday you testified that after the defendant had been subdued in the store, you and the other officer dragged him out on the sidewalk. Is that correct?

McCOLE: No, sir. I said he walked out. He was not dragged out.

Lynn let that roll around in his memory for a moment. Didn't McCole say "dragged"? He was almost certain of it, enough so that he toyed with the notion of asking the court reporter to reread the record. There were, however, certain complications—for one thing, there was a different reporter, creating difficulties in finding the quote; for another, he felt such a probe might prove petty and tiresome to the court, a risk he did not wish to take.

McCOLE: We had him under both arms, but he was walking. He wasn't dragged.

It was important, however, that Lynn pursue the violence of the treatment of his client, regardless of the cause. If he could show that the police were, indeed, brutal . . .

LYNN: Did he fall to the sidewalk at any time?

McCOLE: Not to the best of my knowledge, no.

LYNN: What did you do when you walked him out on the sidewalk?

McCOLE: We put him in a radio car and went to the 79th Precinct.

LYNN: You say you put him in the car. Was he sitting or lying down?

McCOLE: He was sitting.

LYNN: Where was he sitting?

McCOLE: In the rear.

LYNN: He wasn't lying down in the rear?

McCOLE: No, sir.

LYNN: Didn't you have to force his leg into the patrol car?

McCole: Not that I remember, sir.

According to McCole, all they did was hit Blutcher a few times, just to subdue him, put handcuffs on him, then gently escort him to the patrol car. Let the jury absorb that testimony, Lynn thought. Then let them hear what the Trottas had seen.

Lynn pursued this line of attack relentlessly. At one point, it led to a dramatically inspired question.

Lynn: Did he talk to any officer in the Precinct?

McCole: No, sir.

Lynn: No statement was taken from him there?

McCole: He refused to answer, sir.

Lynn: Were you watching him at that time?

McCole: Yes, sir.

Lynn: Was he *able* to answer?

Again, Greenberg was on his feet, his objection sharply interrupting the testimony. And again, he was sustained. Lynn kept right on him, moving the narrative ahead to the hospital.

Lynn: Did you observe him handcuffed in the bed?

McCole: He was on a stretcher, if that's what you consider a bed, and he was handcuffed. . . . We were asked to remove them by the doctor. We took them off at one spell, kept one cuff on, and put one onto the side of the stretcher.

Lynn: The one that was on the side of the stretcher, was that attached to him, also?

McCole: Yes, sir, one was attached to the railing and one was attached to his hand.

Lynn: Then he was shackled in the bed?

Greenberg called out his objection to this choice of words, and again the judge sustained it. Lynn left his stand by the jury box, satisfied. "That is all," he said.

Greenberg returned to face his witness for a few more questions, ostensibly to re-establish, for the jury, the reliability of this police officer and the accuracy of his testimony.

Greenberg: Do you have your memorandum book on the day of December 3, 1967, with you?

McCole: I do, sir.

Greenberg: In your book did you make notations about the weather?

McCole: Yes, sir.

Greenberg: You have a notation?

McCole: Yes, sir.

Greenberg: What was the weather on that day?

McCole (reading): Sunny.

He then asked McCole if the commanding officer of the 79th Precinct, Captain Charles Henry, issued any orders with respect to Sabbath violations, and McCole replied that the captain had done so.

Greenberg: Pursuant to that order, what did you do?

McCole: We checked to see what stores were open and we issued summonses for the violations.

Greenberg: That is all.

It was a slick little package. Two patrolmen were simply following their captain's orders on a nice, clear winter day, right out in the open, presumably with any number of passers-by in the streets. What could be more legitimate than that?

Lynn, seeing McCole with his notebook in hand, decided to see what he could make of it. A fishing campaign, as it were. He began by asking McCole whether he had been on duty in Sector C the previous March, the month in which Blutcher had remembered the first shakedown.

McCole: What day?

Lynn: Any time in March 1967.

McCole: I have to refresh my memory on March, if you like.

Lynn: Yes, do you have it there?

McCole: I would have to go through all of March.

At this point, Greenberg objected, stating that it was too remote and therefore irrelevant. The judge thought otherwise. He instructed the witness to read through his notes from day to day, and "if you find any day in March where you were assigned to Sector C . . . just give those dates, if any." McCole appeared somewhat incredulous for a moment, then, with a shrug, began fumbling through the pages of his aged and somewhat tattered notebook. It was a curious moment in the court, silent except for the occasional sound of his rustling paper, suddenly suspenseful for no reason that anyone could define.

Lynn stood patiently in front of the witness chair, his eyes fixed on McCole like one who expected to shock the jury with some startling confession, and the jury watched, sitting perfectly still, twelve seated statues, watching as McCole kept turning pages, running his eyes down each one, conscious that all eyes were on him, yet not the least perturbed. Across the room, Larry Blutcher watched in bewilderment, somewhat frightened by this turn in the action because there was nothing to be gained from it, nothing at all; Lynn was barking up the wrong tree, it wasn't McCole who had been around in March, it was Repaci. And even if it had been McCole, was he going to admit it? Was he going to admit anything like that? It was almost four minutes before McCole completed his reading. He looked up at Lynn with the same cool, competent, self-assured stare and made his statement.

"No, sir, I was never assigned there in March."

Lynn smiled and thanked him for his efforts. He could only speculate on what he himself might find if he had access to that notebook. However, it was McCole's, and the law stated that the court had no right to it. It was up to McCole to use it as he saw fit, the same way he could use his memory as he saw fit. Conveniently, it helped McCole remember nothing that would incriminate him or run counter to the prosecution's case—as Lynn well knew it would. Lynn's purpose, then, was not to expose the truth —he knew that would be impossible—it was merely to suggest to the jury how completely impossible it was for the defense to elicit the truth from the police.

The Court Follower was very impressed by this maneuver. "Now, that was pretty clever. Lynn had the cop looking through that book, yet everyone in that court knew, no matter what was written in it, he wasn't going to tell you what he didn't want you to know. The funny thing was, you watched the cop fingering through it, and suddenly you got the feeling that he found this act amusing. He was looking through those pages and seeing nothing. Nothing at all. It was all just pretending. If you exposed that book to the court, it would probably have nothing but a lot of doodles in it, or maybe some obscene pictures he'd scrawled in there, or whatever. . . ."

It was 12:25 when Greenberg called Patrolman Philip Repaci to the stand. He came in slowly, watching the floor as he carefully manipulated his crutches by the rear benches, through the maze of tables and chairs that led to the witness stand, quietly refusing all offers of help from sympathetic bystanders. He was dressed in a bright lavender shirt, open at the collar, and when he finally seated himself, he leaned his crutches against the side of the chair like one who hated the very thought of them. There was an appealing quality about him, his stoicism despite all the pain he had suffered, his youthful cheerfulness for all his incapacity. He sat there chewing gum like an impish boy, his pleasant face resembling movie actor John Garfield in his prime, and when he spoke, his manner was gentle and friendly, with no trace of deviousness in his tone. Where McCole demonstrated a stern, mature competence as a witness, Repaci appeared young and ingenuous. It was immediately clear that he would be another superior witness for the prosecution. It seemed most unlikely that such a man could have executed the beating in the first place. And certainly not without terrible provocation.

Greenberg led Repaci through a brief survey of his history. He had been a policeman for six and a half years, five of which had been with the 79th Precinct. He had been crippled as a result of an automobile accident while on duty, an accident—Greenberg magnanimously pointed out—that had nothing to do with this case.

And then he got down to basics:

GREENBERG: Prior to December 3, 1967, had you ever been inside that grocery store?

REPACI: I was never in that store.

GREENBERG: Prior to December 3, 1967, had you ever spoken with him?

REPACI: No, sir.

GREENBERG: In your prior tours, had you ever worked on a Sunday that had the sector where 960 Lafayette Avenue was located?

REPACI: Yes.

GREENBERG: On your prior tours on Sunday, was that store open or closed?

REPACI: I can't recall if it was open on any other Sunday except on that one Sunday.

GREENBERG: In the week prior, seven days prior to December 3, had you observed the store?

REPACI: Yes. . . . I don't recall what days I observed it, but I observed it—what I did know was that the store is open on a Monday.

GREENBERG: That you're sure of?

REPACI: Yes, I am.

Here again, Lynn noted, was another false interpretation of the Sabbath Law, namely, that if a store were closed on a Monday—or, presumably, any other day in the week—it could be opened on Sunday. Blutcher himself had been led to believe this through earlier confrontations with the police, and, as previously noted, had closed his store on a succession of Mondays prior to December 3. However, also as noted, the last Monday in November, immediately prior to the incident, was a date on which welfare checks were distributed to a large number of his creditors; Blutcher could not afford to remain closed on such a day.

The DA proceeded to lead Repaci through his own narrative of the events of that Sunday morning, step by step, starting with the first visit of the radio car to the still-locked grocery store, through the second confrontation that led to the beating. Repaci told exactly the same account that the court had heard from McCole. It was, once again, a convincing twenty minutes of testimony in which Repaci's whole attitude suggested that it was all a very routine incident, properly handled by himself, McCole, and the supervising Sergeant Gallante, in which the principal violence had been instigated by the defendant with his extreme profanity and subsequent physical attack. In fact, he seemed unable to understand what all this hoopla was about.

The one-two punch of McCole and Repaci had been a powerful opening for the prosecution, and Lynn knew there was little he could do in cross-examination to shake it. He concentrated, instead, on reaffirming his question as to their interpretation of the Sabbath Law, another effort to convince the court that the defendant had violated no law to begin with, that the resulting confrontation was therefore entirely out of order.

LYNN: In the Police Academy did you learn anything about violations of grocery stores when they opened for business on Sunday?

REPACI: Yes.

Repaci appeared to be smiling at the question, and for an instant, it appeared to startle Lynn. (Later, Lynn would remember the witness's amusement, speculating on the possible reason for it: "Sabbath Law violations offer a well-known device for dishonest policemen to make a few extra dollars. One can guess that, even in the Police Academy, this is known to recruits. I have heard of instances where patrolling officers make a series of stops at neighborhood groceries within their patrol areas to pick up 'a little of that Sabbath money.' ")

And later:

LYNN: When you began your tour of Sector C, was it your understanding that grocery stores open on the Sabbath were violating the law?

REPACI: Yes.

188

Lynn also tried to get Repaci to admit that in the course of his many tours of duty in Sector C, starting in February 1967, he had observed Blutcher's store open on Sunday and had, as a result, entered that store. Repaci, of course, denied it. If he had passed the store any number of times, he insisted that he was never conscious of its being open. Lynn challenged that, finding it difficult to believe: the store was open for, say, fifty consecutive Sundays and Repaci never once went inside that store to check that so-called violation? The more specific Lynn became about dates, the more evasive were Repaci's replies. He simply did not recall when he had first noticed the store, it could have been any month in the year, and he had absolutely no recollection of its being open on a Sunday before the date of the indictment.

For example:

LYNN: At any rate, you did not observe him open on any Sunday prior to December 3, 1967; is that correct?

REPACI: I do not recall.

LYNN: In other words, you *may* have seen him open?

GREENBERG: Objection, Your Honor, to the phrase "in other words."

JUDGE CORSO: Sustained.

Lynn rephrased the question:

LYNN: Is it possible that you *did* see him open on a Sunday prior to December 3, 1967?

GREENBERG: Objection. Your Honor, the witness answered, he does not remember.

JUDGE CORSO: Sustained.

It was almost one o'clock, and the judge declared a luncheon recess until 2:15.

Mrs. Epsie Blutcher sat through the morning session with her older son John, her attention glued to the presence of Patrolman Repaci. This was the one who had pistol-whipped Larry's head into a bloody pulp. She had never seen him before, but had heard his name often enough. Repaci, Repaci, Repaci. It had long since become a sinister sound in her mind, and now, finally, there he was. The trouble was, he seemed so frail with his crutches and gentle boyish face, so much more like a victim than a villain. She could not help it, but it crossed her mind that it had to be the punishment of God Himself that had crippled this man for life. Like Larry, she could almost feel sorry for him.

Then he began to tell about her son, how he had cursed him, how he had called him such foul things as "white motherfucker," how he had refused to obey "white man's laws." She listened in horror, suppressing an accumulating series of protesting grunts and moans. Was it really Bubba that this man was talking about? Would Bubba ever say words like that? She was not so naïve that she could not understand the reasons for what Repaci was saying, but the whole scene, in this majestic American court of law, bewildered her. She had brought up her children to be God-fearing and law-abiding. They respected the law. They lived decently and honestly by the white man's laws, every one of them. But now it was the white man's policeman, the man who had taken money from her son (she remembered how Bubba had first told her about this, months before December 3), the man who had almost killed her son. *This* was the man who had violated the white man's laws. Yet there he sat, turning the truth of the story upside down, denying that he had ever seen Bubba before, and the jury listened, and the judge listened, nobody said anything, it just went on and on.

When Larry Blutcher met his mother and brother in the hall outside the courtroom, he, too, was feeling the sting of the constantly repeated testimony against him. Over and over, the policemen had made him seem like a pariah and it frightened him. He stood there with his girl and his family, and together they tried to cheer each other up. It would be his turn on the stand soon enough. He would tell the court what really happened, and everything would end up fine. However, when Repaci and McCole passed by, they were joined now by Sergeant Gallante, and Larry could not help but wince at the power lined up against him. Apparently, the sergeant was going to testify, too, another actor in what Larry called "the well-rehearsed play they were putting on."

"Are the Trottas here?" he asked Monica.

She shook her head. Not yet. She had left the courtroom several times during the morning testimony thinking that perhaps they were wandering around the halls, not knowing where to find the courtroom. But she had not seen them. And when they all came back from lunch, there was still no sign of them. The Blutchers milled around, waiting for the bailiff to announce the start of the afternoon sessions, and though no one said anything about it, each of them kept returning his glance toward the elevators.

After the lunch break, the judge had been told of the presence of the defendant's family and had somehow been led to believe that Larry's brother John, among others, was to be called as a witness for the defense. Before opening court for the afternoon sessions, he gave warning: "If there are any people in this courtroom who will at some time or another be called upon to testify, they will not be permitted to testify if they remain in the courtroom. Some of these people sat here through the morning sessions."

Conrad Lynn was embarrassed by this obvious impropriety, or at least, the judge's understanding of it. And though he did not know if he would be calling either brother John or the mother, he left the defense table and asked them to wait outside. They did so, but with extreme reluctance.

"May the record show," Greenberg stated in the curious redundant jargon of lawyers, "none of the People's witnesses were in the courtroom at any time and none of them have left at this point because they're not here."

Mrs. Blutcher, however, had not come to the trial to sit outside the courtroom. Neither, in fact, had John. They had no idea that they were there to be witnesses; they had come to experience the effecting of justice upon their kin. Nor did it help them that a few feet away, the policemen stood chatting in what appeared to be amusement at the whole day's work. Mrs. Blutcher simply did not think she could sit out there, hearing nothing, saying nothing, while the trial progressed.

A few minutes later, Lynn's cross-examination of Patrolman Repaci continued, concentrating on the cause of the fractured thumb, challenging the witness to admit that it might have happened during the beating rather than at the alleged throwing of the pickle jar. In fact, according to the medical report of a Doctor Uic at Cumberland Hospital and the police medical report itself, taken at the 79th Precinct shortly after the incident, it appeared that the injury was typical of the kind sustained during a skirmish such as Repaci had had with Blutcher. Lynn succeeded in getting Repaci to admit that, as he struck the defendant with his gun in his right hand, he was holding the victim with his left, therein rendering the left thumb vulnerable.

It was, however, something less than a major victory.

The prosecution then summoned its last witness, Police Sergeant Joseph Gallante. The court was not surprised when he told exactly the same story that it had already heard several times. And when Conrad Lynn cross-examined, once again he concentrated on the false interpretation of the Sabbath violation, suggesting again to the court that no such violation had occurred.

When Greenberg returned for further direct examination, he buttressed his position in this matter:

GREENBERG: Sergeant, do you recall the defendant saying anything to you about him being closed on any other day than Sunday?

GALLANTE: Patrolman McCole had not said anything. Patrolman Repaci—I questioned him whether he [Blutcher] had closed on any other day and he told me 'no.'

When Gallante was excused the People closed its case. As was typical procedure, the judge immediately recessed the jury for a discussion of law with the two attorneys in the event that the defense wished to offer a motion to dismiss.

During this transition, in the hall out front, Mrs. Blutcher sat waiting with John, suffering increasing anguish at their exclusion from the court. It was, in fact, more than she was able to cope with. Minutes had dragged on, an endless stretch of time that stripped them of conversation, and she had languished on that hard wooden bench trying to pretend that those policemen were not standing there, inescapably in her line of vision, or that their muffled voices did not irritate her ears. She had seen Gallante come out, greeted by the other two, and read into their amusement all the contempt of her victimized son that she had seen in the courtroom. What new things had happened in there? What had this one said? Her sense of fairness was being violated by her exclusion. Was it not *her* son who was on trial? To deny her the right to see and hear it all was, to her, a denial of her motherhood. It was her nature to abide by the judge's ruling, however unreasonable it seemed, but her anxiety had become overwhelming. So, when she heard someone say the word "Recess," she rose with John and together they returned to the court.

They could not have chosen a more inauspicious moment.

Lynn was offering a motion to the court, a motion to dismiss the complaint against the defendant upon the grounds that the prosecution had failed to prove a prima facie case. What had excited him, however, was the strength of his interpretation of the law. He had long since uncovered what he considered to be a basic flaw in the prosecution's case, and he had nursed it through the proceedings until this moment, letting his anticipation build until he could almost taste a possibility of total victory. There was nothing particularly brilliant about it. In fact, it was all so simple he could not see how it could ever be denied.

The basis for his motion, Lynn was explaining to the judge, ". . . is the circumstances of the arrest. Firstly, I do not believe the prosecution has shown in any way that there was any justification for the police entering the premises and telling the defendant that they were going to issue a summons, because the sections of the General Business Law that apply—"

It was at this point that the judge's eye rested upon Mrs. Blutcher and John, and he slammed his open hand on the desk with a sudden, startling display of anger. "Just a minute. If that gentleman over there takes the stand, I tell you right now, you're going to be held in contempt of court!"

Immediately Greenberg was on his feet. "Would you ask the gentleman to identify himself by name?"

Lynn wheeled, befuddled by the suddenness of this interruption. It cut into his concentration with the brusqueness of a thunderclap in the midst of sleep.

"John Blutcher," came the voice from the rear.

"He's the brother of the defendant," Lynn explained.

The judge appeared to struggle with the intensity of his rage. "Look, Mr. Lynn, you are an excellent lawyer, a very honorable lawyer . . . but this court does not like contemptuous action by people . . . I wish you would instruct these people that this judge demands respect. If they dare stick their noses in this courtroom, even if we're not in session, I will hold them in contempt!"

Mrs. Blutcher was as stunned by the intensity of the judge's attack as she was confused by the cause of it. The thought that she had, perhaps, done damage to her son's cause was more painful than the indignity of this complaint against her conduct. She was momentarily too ashamed even to look at Larry, and she rose from her seat to depart as directly as she could. When she returned to the hard, flat bench in the hall, once again in the presence of the three policemen, she resisted any show of the anguish and humiliation she felt so that they might not have cause to revel in it.

Lynn suffered through the resulting lecture and could not help apologizing with as much humility as he could muster. He wanted to be done with this interruption as quickly as possible, for his mind was still bubbling with the juices of his pending triumph. The judge responded in kind, apologizing in turn for having interrupted him.

Lynn picked up where he had left off.

"Now, Your Honor, as I was saying, there is no testimony to show that this defendant was breaking the law . . . As a matter of fact, it is very plain from Section 9 of the General Business Law that he had a right to have his store open for the purpose of selling a long list of foods for the entire day and . . . there was nothing in any testimony by anybody to show that he was selling anything else. So I submit that there was, in the first place, *no* basis for coming in and accusing the defendant of breaking the law."

He paused here, allowing a moment for the court to digest this while he returned to the defense table to pick up the law book out of which he could cement his position. When he returned to his stand before the bench, there was a fresh, strong quality to his voice, and the words came tumbling out of him with a power that was far greater than he had shown during the cross-examinations.

"Now to get to the prosecution's main position . . . when the officers allegedly asked for his name and he did not give it to them and they used the force necessary to arrest him, that force was justified and he [Blutcher] would be responsible in law for any resistance, now I submit that that position is contrary to Section 35.30 of the Penal Law, Subdivision 3, and I read this, if the Court please . . ."

The judge nodded, delaying the reading so that he might refer to his own text to follow Lynn's reading.

For the purposes of this section, a reasonable belief that a person has committed an offense means a reasonable belief in facts or circumstances which, if true, would in law constitute an offense. If the believed facts or circumstances would *not* in law constitute an offense, an erroneous though not unreasonable belief that the law is otherwise *does not render justifiable* the use of physical force to make an arrest . . . [Italics mine. —E.A.]

It was here that the judge stopped him, obviously bewildered by the discrepancy of what he was hearing as against what was before him in his law book.

"Mr. Lynn, where did you read from?"

"Subdivision 3 of 35.30 of the Penal Law, and it is entitled Use of Physical Force to Effect an Arrest.

"May I see that please, because it doesn't seem to jibe with what I have here?"

Lynn offered his law book, and when the judge examined it, he saw the basis for Lynn's startling maneuver. He was, in fact, so impressed that he looked over at Greenberg with a smile that suggested a challenge and addressed his remark to the DA.

"The difficulty here seems to be that I am reading from the current section as amended in laws of March 21, 1968. . . . But what Mr. Lynn just said was the law on the date of this occurrence!"

This was, of course, the essence of Lynn's point: the defendant was being tried ex post facto, and therefore the case against him ought to be dismissed.

"Therefore, Judge, because of that section, the defendant, certain that he had not violated the law, had the right to resist to prevent being taken unjustifiably into custody. According to the officers, just the fact that this man had an open store, just that fact alone, because the officers didn't show anything else, they only showed there was an open store, and one officer, McCole, testified that he saw a person leaving the store with a package. He didn't say what was *in* the package . . . Therefore, the State, having the burden of proof, they would have to show more than what was shown, because the law says it was perfectly legal for a grocery store to be open and to sell a long list of foods. For a policeman to have a belief which would be reasonable, he would have to have something before his eyes which would indicate to him that there had been a selling of some goods which were not legally sold on Sundays. That was left out of the case. . . .

196

"Therefore, the State has not established a prima facie case of the guilt of this defendant."

Lynn stopped, watching the judge for the flavor of his response. There was no doubt that he had surprised him. Lynn contained his smile, walked slowly back to the defense's table, not even bothering to glance at Greenberg. Indeed, he felt like one who had completely turned the tables and upset the entire structure of the prosecution's case.

The judge tapped his pencil on his note pad and looked hard at Greenberg. "I'll hear the District Attorney," he said. He seemed amused at the prospects. How was Greenberg going to wriggle out of this one?

Greenberg began his rejoinder like a desperate man swatting at a mosquito in a dark room. He admitted that "you have a very fine issue here," but he insisted that the defendant "should not be put in the position of judge and jury in the streets of the City of New York." If the officers believed that an offense had been committed, does the defendant have the right "to fight everybody off who is going to try to serve him with the summons"?

Lynn rose to his feet, appalled at this reasoning. The point was, at the time of the incident, the law clearly stipulated that to resist was entirely in order; Greenberg was doing nothing more than stating the case for the repeal of such a law—which was, indeed, effected several months later.

Greenberg, however, kept hammering away, spraying out interpretations of law until, he hoped, he could zero in on the one that would work for him.

"The People take the position that the officers had a right to issue a summons. What the eventual outcome of the summons would be, I don't know. Assume the defendant could beat the charge, assuming he had enough facts on his side and the police couldn't bring enough facts on their side to show that he was actually in violation. We are not here determining a violation of a Sabbath summons. We are here deciding an assault case and resisting arrest. At the time the men tried to serve him with a summons, they weren't adjudicating the case. All they were doing was bringing him to court, not arresting him, not taking him into custody. The defendant by his actions tried to prevent the officers from even serving the summons. He resisted that process. At that point, they had no choice but to take him into custody for the purpose of identifying him. They were arresting him for a Sabbath violation, but he left them no choice but to place him under arrest to determine who he was. He wouldn't identify himself . . ."

As sometimes happens, in his rambling he had stumbled into focus. He saw that now. He had finally found a basis for his rejoinder and he settled on it. "Now, any justification that the defendant may have had to resist an unlawful arrest doesn't come into play because the arrest is not occasioned by the Sabbath violation. The arrest is occasioned by the defendant and his activities after that. Merely asking for a man's name is no reason for having the man now take physical action against the police officers . . . The arrest was occasioned by the fact that he was fighting with the police officers. . . . The defendant had no right to resist at that point because he wasn't being placed under arrest."

The judge nodded, and after considering the matter during a moment's silence, he made his pronouncement: "At this time, decision is reserved on that motion." Then he added: "If between now and prior to the final submission of this case, either side wants to present any authorities to me . . . I shall be happy to consider them."

The Court Follower actually burst out laughing. Not so loudly that it would embarrass the court, but sufficient to jar those who were sitting near him on the spectators' benches. "Lynn was brilliant. He had set them all up, for two days of testimony, he had set them up perfectly, the judge included, and they had fallen right into his trap. There was no doubt about it, he had slapped them down with one good swipe. First with the Sabbath Law.

Nobody had known what it was until he told them. The cops, the DA, even the judge, I'll bet. The DA himself, he said it: you can't open on Sunday. The cop had said it: he wasn't closed on Monday, so he couldn't open on Sunday. All nonsense. They didn't know the law. How do you like that, they didn't know the law they were arresting him for! Lynn had thrown it right in their faces: those cops had no right to be in that store at all.

"And then the second part, the right to resist arrest under the old law, that was really beautiful. The DA looked like he'd just swallowed a turd. And the judge, he kept shaking his head with that silly little grin. He was shocked, all right. He didn't know what to do!"

To Blutcher, the defendant, the arguments spun around him in a way that made no sense. "If someone was to ask me I'd say this whole thing is crazy. I mean, they're doing all that arguing back and forth about something that didn't happen that way at all. The DA talks like it wasn't me who got hurt, it was Repaci's thumb. I don't know anything about Repaci's thumb. I didn't resist arrest. They came into my store and they asked me for money. I never threw any punches. I never threw a pickle jar. It's crazy: the DA asks Repaci, Did you take money from this man?—like all you had to do was ask and Repaci would say 'Yeah, and when he wouldn't give me any, I pistol-whipped him.' I mean, man, it's crazy!

"Then the DA is saying, well, okay, the law says maybe I could resist arrest, but I can't resist a summons. But the way it works, I'd like to know the difference. You take the summons, then you've got to go to court. If you plead not guilty like they say I could, then you've got to go back to court maybe a dozen times. That's the way it works. That's the way they run it. Everybody knows that. They run it that way so the next guy won't try to buck the system. But if you try, that means you got to sacrifice your business or your job. Sure, if you finally win, you don't have to pay the five dollars. But you have to pay your lawyer and it cost you maybe twenty or thirty hours from work, and all you've won is that you don't have to pay the five dollars you shouldn't have been charged with in the first place.

"Then the real wild part is, you could bet the cops will be back the next Sunday and the whole thing will start all over again."

Nonetheless, Blutcher was fascinated. He was enjoying the importance of being in the center of it all, all those people, all this attention, all dedicated to him. He would watch the jury as they listened to what was being said about him, and he maintained his confidence that they would find him innocent. If the machinations of the DA and the judge bewildered him, he had complete respect for his attorney. Even the deference that the judge had accorded Mr. Lynn impressed him; he felt that Mr. Lynn's prominence was a reflection on him as well.

"Mr. Lynn seemed very hopeful, and so did I. I mean, I just couldn't see all those jury people believing those lies about me. White or black, that just couldn't matter. Mr. Lynn said he didn't think the DA believed the lies, either. What we needed was to tell them all the truth, and to make sure the Trottas were there to tell what they had seen. That was very important, he made that clear to me. I should go to their place early in the morning and pick them up myself, and bring them to court myself."

For the following day, Wednesday, June 11, would be Blutcher's day in court.

15

It was late afternoon when Lynn returned to his office in lower Manhattan. He immediately began preparing a memorandum to dismiss the indictment, concentrating on finding precedents for the defendant's right to resist unjustifiable approach and arrest by police officers. There were a number of cases to support this; outstanding among them was People vs. Singleton, dated 1952, which closely approximated the facts as alleged in People vs. Blutcher. As he wrote in his memo: "A police officer investigating a report of a commotion, entered the defendant's apartment. The defendant was not engaged in any wrongdoing, and when the officer refused to leave, the defendant bloodied the officer's lip in an attempt to push him out of the apartment. Since the officer was not about a lawful duty, the Court held that the defendant was justified in using force to protect himself and eject the officer from the premises. . . . In another case, People vs. Cherry, two police in plain clothes grabbed the defendant on a darkened street. He fought back, injuring one of the officers. He was charged with assault. The court ruled in part:

> . . . whether or not defendant believed that they were police officers, he had a right to resist, and that quite apart from any fear or threat of physical harm and injury. For most people, an illegal arrest is an outrageous affront and intrusion—the more offensive because it is under cover of law—to be resisted as energetically as a violent assault.

"Herein, again, the court reversed the conviction of the defendant."

But times had changed since these rulings were made. In the last several years, crime had become a major political and moral issue, especially in urban areas where the ills and tensions of society were normally concentrated. It was no sudden insight that brought the New York State Legislature to amend its Penal Law in March 1968, stripping the citizen of his right to resist unlawful arrest: it was another submission to the public pressure for a more-power-to-the-police solution. As Assistant DA Greenberg had so bluntly put it: ". . . the defendant should not be put in the position of being judge and jury in the streets of the City of New York." If that were, in fact, a gross overstatement of the victim's prerogative, even according to pre-March 1968 law, the direct opposite had been the result of the new law. It has already been noted how, in the election of the previous year, the voters in New York City had renounced the participation of even a minority of distinguished citizens on the Police Civilian Complaint Review Board. And now, as Lynn had repeatedly pointed out during his examination of jurors during the impaneling, there was a consistent emphasis on the same police-power, law-and-order solutions to the problems of crime during the 1969 Mayorality primary campaigns then in full swing.

It was in this area that Lynn saw the real truth that gave this trial its significance. It was, actually, the most important reason he had consented to undertake the defense in a case that seemed infinitely less consequential and financially rewarding than his time and energy would normally permit. He wanted to show the courts that not all black people were *ipso facto* criminals when they came into conflict with police power, that when the civilian gave up his rights as a sacrifice to his fear of crime, he might well suffer another kind of crime from his so-called guardians.

As he wrote his memorandum, Lynn could not help but speculate that the judge might dismiss the case. If not, it would certainly affect his charge to the jury when he sent them out to reach a verdict.

Of one thing he was absolutely certain: he had shaken up the court. He went home that night pleased with the prospects of the coming day.

The Court Follower lived in Brooklyn Heights, a pleasant walk from the Civic Center. "I kept thinking of that McCole on the stand, the way he had fingered through his notebook and my own notions of what might have been written in it. Like the way the DA had asked him what was the weather on that Sunday, the way he checked and said, 'Yeah, it was sunny,' merely to show the jury how precise it all was. It was as if he had recorded everything, that he could tell you how many beers he'd had the night before.

" 'It was sunny.' December 3, 1967. It stuck in my craw, the way he'd said that. "Well, Sunday, it was a football day. Were the Jets home that Sunday? As soon as I got home I checked my son's scrapbook (his huge, newspaper-sized, Superbowl-Joe Namath-covered scrapbook). December 3, 1967.

"Well, there it was, and it broke me up: DENVER BRONCOS UPSET JETS, 33-24. Four Namath passes intercepted. Only 32,903 showed up and sat through a *steady rain!*

"There was a picture, too. The loyal fans at Shea Stadium under all those umbrellas, and the field was a sea of mud. I remembered that game. I was one of the loyal wet ones. I remembered the day, rain from morning on. Rain so steady my wife said I'd be crazy to go, fighting about taking the boy, the same old female nonsense . . .

" 'It was sunny,' McCole had said.

"Sure, that must be one helluva notebook."

On Tuesday night, from still another city, there was another report of the polluted atmosphere, as Conrad Lynn had put it. The juries of America were working overtime for the police. It was the time of the cop:

THREE CHICAGO POLICEMEN ACQUITTED IN THE BEATING OF A NEWSMAN.

So went the radio news. The *New York Times* reported the jury trial of police brutality relating to the clubbing of a reporter during the demonstrations accompanying the Democratic National Convention in Chicago. "This will give the Chicago police department assurance that in the performance of their duty they will not be exposed to [further] federal prosecutions such as this," defense attorney George B. Crowly commented. Judge Perry, presiding, had told the jury that there had been ample provocation. "The victim had charged some of these officers with incest with their mothers. It was so provocative, any red-blooded American would have flared up. They then got excited and used excessive force."

"Incest with their mothers . . ." Lynn played around with the phrase, appalled that a judge would appraise a federal case around a frequently heard profanity. If a cop called a civilian a motherfucker, would that equally justify an assault on the cop? Would Judge Perry appraise it so? Lynn was no student of Freudian psychology, but he knew that cops had always been regarded as father-figures. Might he not ask (albeit whimsically), did not that legitimately qualify cops as motherfuckers? The rhetoric of our times lent itself to all sorts of absurdities . . .

The Trottas. The Trottas. Wednesday, June 11, did not begin auspiciously for Larry Blutcher. He and Monica appeared at the

Trotta apartment a few minutes after eight, allowing plenty of time to take them to the Civic Center and its Supreme Court Building. However, no one was home. Or, at least, no one answered the door. They rang persistently for over ten minutes without success. They went outside to a phone booth and called, and again, no one responded. Somewhat desperate now, they decided that Monica would wait at the apartment while Larry went to Bernard Trotta's place of work, the Western Carpet Company. If, by nine o'clock, no one answered or showed up at the apartment, Monica would go to Dexter's school. Then, hopefully, they would all meet at the trial by ten.

It was a wasted effort, and Larry knew it. Even as he scurried from street to street trying to hail a taxi, panic was rising in his throat. Bernard Trotta would not be at work and Dexter would not be in school. Either they had all gone off somewhere or they were hiding in their apartment, not answering the door. It was all there in his past failure to appear, in his false promises, in his all-too-apparent fear of police reprisals. Larry had seen that in an earlier controversy between Trotta and his wife in which she had been the strong one, not he, demanding that he go to testify in defiance of whatever he felt the police might do to them, that blacks should stick together, especially when truth was so much on their side. Then there was that intimidating letter from the New York police headquarters at 100 Centre Street that Trotta said he had received, something to do with his testifying, he told Larry—but when Larry asked to see it, ostensibly to show it to Mr. Lynn, or at least to read it to him, Trotta never seemed to have it with him. All Trotta could say was that he didn't like the whole business, especially that letter. He kept asking, how did the police know he was going to testify?

Blutcher was not surprised, then, when he learned that Trotta had not shown up at work either. It was a few minutes after ten when he finally arrived at the Supreme Court Building, a small part of him still clinging to the hope that the Trottas would be there waiting for him, and his eyes swept the busy lobby on the ground floor as he entered in case they had forgotten where to go —though he had told them several times—then eagerly went up the elevator to the seventh floor and the long broad hall that led to Room 741, with the more reasonable hope that they would be there, outside the door, where they had actually promised to be.

No, it was too much to ask; and he sat down on the bench with his mother and brother John, and a few minutes later, his sister Vina, and even a few young boys from John's organization, Together We Stand, all dressed up in military style; it all seemed so silly to Larry, so feeble, so pitifully inadequate.

"It was like this was all part of the same scene, the way they've got us whipped. There was just the three cops there, they didn't even have to wear their uniforms, they stood there talking and kidding around, and they were getting paid their wages for the day, just as much for coming here as for riding patrol. They had taken my money, beaten me up, and arrested me for assault, and just because they could do that to us, Trotta was too scared to come to testify that that is exactly what they do. I thought, then, heck, I couldn't really blame him, he was like most of the old black people, they had been beaten on for so long, they were contented to take whatever little bit they had and pray to the fair-haired Jesus that nobody would take it away from them."

The trial reopened on Wednesday. The DA wished to make an application concerning a point of law related to Conrad Lynn's memorandum. It was over this somewhat startling statement by Lynn that Greenberg was worried, and the judge was all too ready to listen. So it was that when the jury entered, it was again immediately dismissed.

It was at this time that Blutcher, keeping one eye on the door, saw Monica come in, and though he had long since abandoned hope that the Trottas would show up, he found himself begging that somehow she had found them, even just little Dexter, and he watched her move to a vacant seat near his mother, waiting for the instant when their eyes would meet. At once, she looked over at him, then shook her head and shrugged, a double negative, as it were. He replied with a gesture of futility and returned his attention to the action in front of the bench.

Greenberg began with an artful humility. "Yesterday, when I addressed myself to the argument, I must admit that I was caught short by Mr. Lynn . . ."—an attitude that indicated he had thought it over during the long night and had resolved the problem to his satisfaction. "Where an officer seeks to make an arrest on grounds that he reasonably believes that he has, the law says if he makes a mistake he may be held responsible—but the mistake is one we must look at very clearly. The mistake is not whether or not the defendant is the actual perpetrator of the crime. The mistake must be to the heart of the crime itself. In other words—taking a very simple illustration—if a man is walking on the street and a police officer in an erroneous belief that walking on the street is a crime, arrests the man for walking on the street, and he's in error . . . then the officer has no right to use force. But if a bank robbery has been committed and the officer has reasonable grounds to believe that this is the man who committed the crime, because bank robbery is a crime, then he seeks to arrest him and has the right to use necessary force. . . . If it turns out the man is not in fact the perpetrator, that doesn't relieve the defendant from the responsibility of his criminal act in resisting the arrest."

The judge, however, was quick to question this interpretation. He pointed out that in the DA's analogy, a felony (bank robbery) had been committed whereas, in this matter, "which is at best a misdemeanor, is not the law somewhat different than a felony, in that the police officer has the right to arrest on a misdemeanor only when that misdemeanor was committed in his presence?"

Greenberg believed that he was speaking with relevance. "The key here is based upon what the officer saw and believed. Did he believe that a crime had been committed for Sabbath Law violation in his presence? The officer walks into an open store. The shelves are stocked. There is a meat counter. There are many articles on display in the store. . . ." Greenberg deferred to precedent with a 1958 case, People vs. Ozer, wherein a patrolman entered a loft premises used for the cutting of men's garments, and he finds therein Mr. Ozer who is in the act of cutting a pair of pants. There are no other people in the place and the officer asks if he can buy a pair of pants—which Mr. Ozer offers to sell him —whereupon Ozer is given a summons. The court, however, ruled in favor of Mr. Ozer: ". . . a private transaction occurring between the parties does not constitute a violation of the Sabbath Law." Greenberg then made his point: "There is no doubt that the loft premises in the Ozer case was not open to the public. There was no exposure of the goods for public use, but [the ruling] lays the groundwork. . . . It defines offering for sale and it defines it as a display for sale in a public place, such as a store. . . . Looking at the record here, we have testimony that there was a meat counter. Granted, there is no testimony as to what was in the meat counter. . . . The record does not show what, if anything, was on the shelves. We know there was a display of pickle jars on the counter. . . ."

Lynn was both amused and distressed by Greenberg's reasoning. His use of the Ozer case, for example, was no more logical than his analogy about the bank robber that the judge had so correctly criticized. That Mr. Ozer had been acquitted because he was *not* displaying goods for public sale does not make Laurence Blutcher guilty merely because he had. Lynn could readily point out that many grocery stores have beer licenses and openly display beer on Sunday, but they do not permit its sale until after one o'clock, the legal time: does Mr. Greenberg suggest that the mere display of the beer justifies an arrest?

All this he was prepared to protest, but as it turned out, Greenberg had a far more damaging play to make.

". . . At this time, the People would ask leave to reopen the People's case for an examination of what was in this store, what was on public display, did any sales take place of merchandise in the presence of any police officer . . . articles that would be in contravention of that section which would give the right for the police officer to serve his summons. . . ."

Lynn was deeply disturbed by such a proposal: "If Your Honor please, I will oppose this application to reopen because the witnesses *were* given full opportunities to describe exactly what they observed and what they considered to be a violation —and in my cross-examination particularly I carefully asked each officer what were the circumstances that caused him to believe that this man was violating the Sabbath, so they have already testified. . . . [Is Mr. Greenberg saying] that any grocery store [which] opens on Sunday legally, say at 1:30 in the afternoon, it must then take all of the stock off its shelves that cannot be sold on that day, hide it in some way, put it in the back room or somewhere, and leave out on the shelves only these articles here that are listed. . . . It cannot be shown that this is a violation of law. I don't know of any case that has held that."

If Lynn was disturbed by Greenberg's proposal, he was shocked at the judge's response.

"Mr. Lynn, aren't we more or less jumping the gun? I think what you are now saying is quite right and it agrees with my thinking, but aren't we rather—let me put it this way—aren't you arguing a point when none of us knows yet what testimony or what the nature or extent of the testimony that the District Attorney will offer?"

(It was the nature of the judge's reasoning that now upset him. It just didn't make sense. The judge was agreeing with him, or so he said, yet wasn't he actually submitting to the DA's request?)

". . . It is within my discretion," the judge went on, "if in the interest of justice on the application of either side that I might permit an advantage in order to afford either side the opportunity of proving additional points . . ."

(And now he was saying that, though he is admittedly going to do the DA a significant favor, he is being completely fair about it, for he would also have done so for the defense.)

"If the court please," Lynn continued his protest, "I can understand and I concede, of course, it is certainly within the discretion of the court to reopen. However, in this instance, the District Attorney is not offering a new witness or new circumstances. It seems to me, if [the three officers] were to testify in addition to the cross-examination in which I tried to find out if there is anything else they observed . . . they would be in conflict with what they have already testified. . . ."

Greenberg, here, interceded: "The People don't intend to produce new witnesses. The People intend to produce new evidence."

And the judge conclusively supported him: "I don't think criminal trials, especially, should be relegated to a game of wits. If something in the interest of a defendant warrants that some of the strict rules of procedure . . . be not strictly followed, believe you me, I will not strait-jacket an attorney on either side. . . ."

Lynn kept shaking off this unctuous protestation of fairness. When one is getting slaughtered by an arbitrary ruling, it is of no satisfaction to hear the referee say that he might just as easily have permitted the same ruling to the other side. "As a matter of fact, Your Honor, since the prosecution has closed its case . . . my defendant is being imperiled since I had proceeded with the confidence that the District Attorney had presented his full case. I feel this is very much against his interests to open the case at this point. It would be different if these officers had been restricted in [their testimony]. . . ."

And once again, the judge agreed, with an additional compliment: "I remember that pretty well, and I can just about visualize your cross-examination of these officers after I grant the motion. . . ." which he then proceeded to do "in the interests of justice," granting to Lynn, for the record, the right to make an exception to his ruling. Lynn, of course, made that exception, and the jury was resummoned.

In the rear, the Court Follower watched in amusement as he saw it all unfold. "Of course, of course. Lynn could have referred to ten straight decisions from the U.S. Supreme Court that declared all police beatings unconstitutional no matter what the provocation, and the judge would not have dismissed the charges. That's the way it works, all right. The cops can do no wrong and no little black sonovabitch is going to get away with bucking *that* system.

"It was a damn good moment, though. Every once in a while you see a DA squirm and the judge squirms with him, and you know that you've seen a good show."

Lynn returned to the defense table somewhat miffed by this defeat, only to learn that the Trottas had failed to appear. ("I felt like a pitcher who had just thrown his best pitch and the umpire had called it a ball, only to turn around then and discover that the outfielders had disappeared.")

And there was Patrolman McCole, back on the witness stand, and Sheldon Greenberg in front of him, probing for the testimony that would help cement his case. If there were any doubts as to whether the DA had met with and coached his witness as to his immediate responsibilities, they were quickly dispelled by McCole's adept references to the matter at hand.

GREENBERG: Would you again give us the description of what you saw with great particularity?

McCOLE: . . . Inside the meat counter were uncooked meats and poultry. Around the store was canned goods and assorted goods on display.

GREENBERG: When you entered, how many people were in the store beside yourself?

McCOLE: Two. There was a boy emerging from the store with packages and a man engaged in a transaction with the defendant.

GREENBERG: The boy coming out of the store with the pack-ages, can you describe the packages?

McCOLE: Just a large package. A bag.

GREENBERG: Then there was a man in the store . . . Can you describe what happened there?

McCOLE: There was canned goods put into a bag, an amount of money went over the counter and then the man left.

GREENBERG: The man took the canned goods with him?

McCOLE: Yes, sir.

GREENBERG: And who took the money?

McCOLE: The defendant.

GREENBERG (to Lynn): Your witness.

Larry Blutcher felt the beginnings of pain in his head. His temples throbbed, just enough to worry him. The Trottas. McCole was talking about the Trottas, spinning out a string of convenient lies. Terrible lies. The truth was, Dexter did not leave before his father. Nor did he carry out a package. His father did not buy canned goods, but merely a package of ciga-rettes. The Trottas. Where were the Trottas? How could McCole make up lies like that unless he knew that the Trottas were not going to testify to the opposite? What's more, there were no "un-cooked meats and poultry" in the meat counter. The refrigera-tion unit had been on the blink for several weeks. That had been one of the elements of his problems—he could not get it fixed. He did not have the cash to do it. He didn't have the cash be-cause he didn't have the stock, and vice versa, and if he had, he would have used that meat counter, he would have stocked it, and maybe he might have felt differently about the Sabbath Law and maybe even paid them off. The irony of McCole's deceit hurt him badly. They were tearing him apart with all those lies.

The trouble was, Lynn could do nothing to shake McCole. He had only his testimony to challenge him on, and the two faced each other in a hair-splitting battle over exactly what McCole had actually seen. It was all fruitless and debilitating. Lynn ended up doing nothing better than to get an admission that

McCole had, indeed, spoken with Greenberg earlier that morning.

If Lynn felt that this was something of a victory, Greenberg quickly dispelled it.

GREENBERG: Patrolman McCole, during your years as a police officer, have you testified in criminal trials?

McCOLE: Yes, sir. Fifty.

GREENBERG: In each of these trials, was the People of the State of New York represented by an Assistant District Attorney?

McCOLE: Yes, sir.

GREENBERG: And prior to testifying at each of these trials, before you got to the stand, did you speak to the Assistant DA?

McCOLE: Yes, sir.

McCole was sitting there, nodding his head slowly, like one who was far more bored with criminal trials than he was with his other police duties. Fifty trials, Lynn mused. He thought of questioning that figure. If McCole had been on the force six years, he would have been involved in a criminal trial on an average of once almost every month. It seemed like a startling figure. Was it a typical one? Or was there something about McCole that brought him to court more frequently than others?

In the end, Lynn decided against pursuing this. He was weary of McCole. The man was beginning to irritate him, upsetting his normal lawyer's courtroom cool. If it could be equally said that Lynn was annoying to McCole, this afforded him no real satisfaction. He had nothing more to ask him, and McCole was dismissed. He could go home and put a fifty-first notch in his belt, Lynn thought.

Once again, the judge accepted the closing of the People's case and deferentially referred to Mr. Lynn's motion, but reserved his decision. Lynn was not surprised. He nodded respectfully, then opened the case for the defense by calling the defendant himself to the stand.

The Court Follower watched Blutcher walk to the witness stand and his years as an observer went to work for him. "I've

213

seen more cases tried than most of the lawyers who try them. It's like a smart football fan who gets to really know the game. It's fourth down and a foot to go at midfield in a close game, and he sees his team going to try for a first down instead of punting. He says, no, don't do it. It won't work. The crowd is yelling, yes, yes, go for it, but the fan knows better, sometimes even better than the coach. . . .

"Well, the way I saw it, putting the defendant on the stand now wasn't going to work. It was going to end up badly. Lynn didn't have to do it. He could have surprised everybody and done absolutely nothing . . ."

16

"It was like walking on stage in a play and you're not sure you know your part. I told myself, I shouldn't be nervous or anything, but I guess I couldn't help it. I was afraid that after all the lies they had told about me, who would believe the truth from me? I mean, you get to thinking, why should they believe me?"

He stood up as straight as his five foot, eight inches could take him. His dark suit was neatly pressed and well-fitted. His tie was properly conservative, not because of the trial, but because that was his style. And on his lapel he wore the red, black, and green emblem that symbolized his African heritage. One could see how he struggled to maintain his poise in the face of this Armageddon, finally, after all these agonizing months of delays and the preceding hours of mendacity. And when he stated his name, his voice seemed to be stopped somewhere in his throat, and to let it out, he expended an excess of power. As a result, the sound of his name rang loudly through the hall, or so it seemed to him, but then he guessed that it was only his imagination, momentarily distorted because of his nervousness.

He sat down in the witness chair so recently warmed by his enemy, the man named McCole, and leaned forward as if to greet the short, black, bearded, friendly figure of his attorney.

"Mr. Blutcher," Lynn began, "we want you to keep your voice up, but you don't have to talk too loudly. Just talk in a normal way. Mr. Blutcher, how old are you?"

"Thirty-two."

"How long have you lived in Brooklyn?"

"About twenty-five years."

He told the court that he had been a paratrooper in the Army and was honorably discharged in 1958. He explained that he went into the grocery business because, ever since he had been a small boy, he wanted to be in business for himself. "I felt that's the only way you could make for yourself was in business." Then he related how he opened the store at 960 Lafayette Avenue, how hard he worked, staying open at times to midnight or later, and how tough the competition was from the larger store directly across the street.

And then Lynn opened the main door: "Did there come a time, Mr. Blutcher, that you were visited by police officers?"

It took a dozen or more questions, interspersed with a few vigorous objections, before Blutcher could spell out his agonies to the court. Yes, he had received his first Sabbath Law violation in February. No, it was not Repaci who had issued it. Repaci had first come around in March, forcing him to pay off or be closed down, and had followed with another visit in June. Then he didn't see Repaci again until November, he could not recall exactly what date, and Repaci had told him he would have to give him a summons for being open on that Sunday "or else you know what you have to do," and Blutcher had done it again, paid him off three dollars, only to have to face him a week later. Blutcher had been closed on that Monday, and so indicated to

Repaci, but in a curious reversal, the policeman told him that being closed on Monday didn't matter, only to reverse himself again on the following week when he drove by on Monday and, seeing the store open, stopped and said: "You're open . . . I'll be back on Sunday!"

And that Sunday was December 3.

It was a frenzied twenty minutes of testimony, most of which kept Greenberg on his feet to object, and the judge poking questions at the witness, and Lynn rephrasing questions like a man with half his mind shackled by legal restrictions. If, in the last analysis, this testimony was finally exposed to the court, it was done at considerable expense to the defendant's equanimity. Blutcher was suffering the all-too-familiar frustrations of eager witnesses, unable to pour out the truth after all the preceding lies. For example, he was driven to blurt out such impermissible statements as: "I know that everybody in the community that had stores was paying the policemen off!" On another occasion he was denied the right to explain what had happened to him in February 1967, when he had received his first summons. The ever-present sight of the DA leaping to his feet intimidated him, kept him on edge. What could he say and what could he not say? They were even objecting to Mr. Lynn's questions. Was it hurting his case before the jury if his testimony was so constantly studded with objections?

Then, finally, they came to the incident of December 3. Lynn was careful to make every point as thoroughly as it had to be made, repeating key questions for proper emphasis, driving home the evidence as seen through the eyes of the victim.

LYNN: Will you tell the jury exactly what happened. Did you see the patrol car come to a stop in front of your door?

BLUTCHER: Yes, it was stopped. Then they got out and came in.

LYNN: You say "they." Two got out?

BLUTCHER: They both got out and came into the store.

LYNN: You heard Patrolman McCole and Patrolman Repaci testify that Repaci came out alone that second time. Do you remember him saying that?

BLUTCHER: Yes, I do.

LYNN: But that is not your recollection?

BLUTCHER: No, it's not true.

LYNN: So what actually happened is that both of these policemen got out of the car; is that right?

BLUTCHER: Yes, that's correct.

LYNN: And then what did they do?

BLUTCHER: They came into the store and Patrolman McCole walked up to the counter and he said to me, he says, "You're going to have to close up the store, otherwise you know what you have to do." . . . And I was saying back, I was saying to them that "I'm not going to pay no policemen off any more" and I said, "The best thing you could do is give me a summons and leave the premises."

LYNN: And what did they say to you, if anything?

BLUTCHER: At that time, Repaci, he hollered out from the background, "You wise bastard," just like that, and so I hollered back and said, "The best thing you could do is give me a summons and leave my premises," and McCole—one of them—went out to call the sergeant out in the squad car.

LYNN: Now, did the officer ask you for your name?

BLUTCHER: They never asked me for my name at all.

LYNN: Then what—

BLUTCHER: Then when McCole came back in, there was a little boy there, Dexter Trotta, he came in to buy a pickle—that's all he bought, just a pickle—and they said, "Get your pickle and leave," and then they locked the door.

LYNN: Then what happened?

BLUTCHER: When the sergeant came, they opened the door and the sergeant came up to the counter where I was standing behind and he asked me what was the matter. He was smiling.

LYNN: Sergeant Gallante, who testified?

BLUTCHER: Yes, Sergeant Gallante. I was saying to him: "I'm not going to pay any cops off. The best thing you could do is give me a summons," and right away Patrolman Repaci said, "You're under arrest," and so I said, "Okay, I'll go downtown with you." So when I came from behind the counter over near where the pickle jars were, they both came over and grabbed me.

LYNN: Then what happened?

BLUTCHER: They threw me down and I couldn't tell exactly what they was beating me with but anyway, he started beating me with something. I thought it was a billy, and he was beating me and beating me; as I laid there bleeding, I guess, when blood started coming, I heard McCole say, "That's enough. Stop beating him!" And Repaci said, "No, I'm going to kill this black mother-fucker!"

LYNN: Now, Mr. Blutcher, did you hear the officers say that you threw a pickle jar at them?

BLUTCHER: Yes, I did.

LYNN: Did you throw a pickle jar at anyone?

BLUTCHER: No, I didn't.

LYNN: Were you near the pickle jar when they grabbed you?

BLUTCHER: Yes, when they grabbed me, all the pickle jars fell down on the floor, because that's where they grabbed from . . . before I got to the end of the counter, they grabbed me and swerved me around, and all the pickle jars fell down on the floor.

LYNN: Did you fight the officers at all?

BLUTCHER: No, I didn't fight—as a matter of fact, they took me by surprise because I was going to go downtown with them. I wasn't putting up any struggle at all. So when they grabbed at me, actually I didn't resist because I went right down, and that's when they started beating me.

LYNN: And did the sergeant say anything at the time?

BLUTCHER: I imagine the sergeant had left, after he saw the blood.

LYNN: But you do not recall him saying anything?

BLUTCHER: No.

LYNN: And on the floor, did they handcuff you?

BLUTCHER: Yes. I was asking them why was they beating me and they said, "Shut up, motherfucker" . . . and then they dragged me to the front of the store and drug me outside.

LYNN: You heard the officers testify you walked out with them.

BLUTCHER: No.

LYNN: That was not true?

BLUTCHER: That was not true.

Here, Greenberg objected once again, claiming it was for the jury to decide what was true or not true. The judge sustained. Lynn was amused by this: the examination must be going extremely well if Greenberg had to go picking at such details.

LYNN: At any time before you had gotten to the patrol car were you standing?

BLUTCHER: No, they shoved me in the patrol car and my leg was hanging out and one of them kicked my leg in. . . .

Blutcher then told of the additional roughing up he received at the 79th Precinct station, the arrival of the ambulance, and his stay in the hospital.

Lynn was finished with his direct examination, but there was one other matter, a delicate matter, and he knew it had to be faced. Before he turned the defendant over to the cross-examination of the DA, he thought it best to question Blutcher on his police record. This, of course, was purely a tactic for the sensitivity of the jury; it was far better to reveal this one's self than to risk letting the DA uncover it.

Greenberg, however, immediately made use of it. He acted as though he had no knowledge of this, though it was, of course, a matter of record. He had barely gotten to his feet when he asked Blutcher: "What were you convicted of?"

BLUTCHER: Attempted assault. [Referring to the plea-bargaining in the matter of Carrie Jones and the statutory rape.]

GREENBERG: Was that assault on a police officer?

BLUTCHER: No. It was attempt to assault.

(This was anything but an explanation, but Greenberg was shrewd enough not to probe any deeper into it.)

GREENBERG: Is that your only conviction?

BLUTCHER: No, it isn't.

GREENBERG: Oh, there's another one?

(Again, he seemed genuinely surprised—like a child being offered a second piece of candy.)

BLUTCHER: Yes.

Here, Greenbert showed the jury his magnanimity by offering to turn this aspect of the examination back to Conrad Lynn. "Do you want to inquire about the other one or shall I?"

Lynn replied that he would be glad to, but what emerged— the policy conviction with its $250 fine, and the other disorderly conduct convictions for crap-shooting—came out sounding far more unseemly than he would have liked.

Greenberg, then, began pecking away at Larry, pricking a dozen little balloons in a way that would have to influence a jury:

GREENBERG: Did you have a fractured skull?

(Lynn had so indicated in his opening statement.)

BLUTCHER: I don't know. It felt like one.

GREENBERG: Any doctor ever tell you you had one?

BLUTCHER: No, no doctor ever told me.

GREENBERG: The summons back in February 1967, were you convicted on that?

BLUTCHER: I paid a fine.

GREENBERG: You pleaded guilty?

BLUTCHER: Yes.

GREENBERG: To what?

BLUTCHER: To Sabbath-breaking.

GREENBERG: Is that the only conviction you had for Sabbath-breaking?

BLUTCHER: Is that the only one I had for Sabbath-breaking?

GREENBERG: Right. That one . . . ?

BLUTCHER: I was given a summons again when I was going back and forth to the courthouse.

GREENBERG: On which charge?

BLUTCHER: I was convicted of Sabbath Law again on this charge.

GREENBERG: On the one of December 3, 1967?

BLUTCHER: Yes. For December 3.

Greenberg appeared to be staggered by this, and kept repeating the question: December 3, 1967, the day everybody is talking about here? Blutcher kept answering, annoyed by the carping. After all, wasn't it in the indictment? Then it became apparent what Greenberg was driving at.

GREENBERG: Did you plead guilty or were you found guilty by a judge?

BLUTCHER: I pleaded guilty.

Again Greenberg all but gasped in surprise, to emphasize its importance. This was the very same Sabbath violation that the defense had been so vigorously contesting as being illegal. Indeed, it was at the essence of Lynn's motion for dismissal. And here the defendant admits that he pleaded guilty to that very same charge.

Lynn shook his head, not just a little dismayed. He had made a mistake. A year before, he had allowed the inefficiency of the courts to wear him down in defense of that summons to his client. He had told Blutcher to pay the five dollars and be done with it. And now the DA was making him pay for it again.

Greenberg then made reference to Blutcher's testimony that the patrolmen had never asked him for his name. Yet, from the Grand Jury testimony in September 1968, he read Blutcher's testimony as follows:

Q: Did they ask you to identify yourself?
A: They said, Identify yourself. I said, My name is on the wall.

Did Blutcher remember giving that testimony?

Larry shook him off. He replied that he *could* have said that because his name *was* on the wall. Greenberg persisted; he was not interested in whether or not his name was on the wall; he was only interested in whether he remembered saying that before the Grand Jury, repeating the question over and over until finally he got Blutcher to admit it.

Greenberg, however, was not relentless. Having accomplished a string of small victories, he chose to conclude his cross-examination with an action of surprising generosity. From the Grand Jury hearing, he also read a lengthy passage of Blutcher's testimony relating to the circumstances of the beating as he had told it then. It was, in effect, so similar to the testimony he had just given on Lynn's direct examination, it must certainly have rung true to the jury. And with that, the DA released the witness.

Immediately thereafter, the judge recessed the trial for lunch. Lynn was returning his papers to his briefcase when the judge called him to the bench. A little informal chat, as it were, the sort of extra-legal conversation that frequently occurs between friendly colleagues. "The judge seemed very concerned. He told me he felt sympathy for the defendant but had no confidence in how the jury would respond. The case had that sort of feel about it; at first it seems to lean one way, then another. He thought that what I needed was a good witness. Why weren't we able to get that witness into court?"

Indeed, there was still an hour and a half to arrange for this, and the defense had every intention of using it. Blutcher was still a little shaky from his hour on the witness stand, but he and Monica hurried into a taxi and returned to Reid Avenue and the Trotta apartment. Others in the Blutcher family made exploratory calls, went to Bernard Trotta's place of work, to young Dexter's school. It was the same as the early morning, however—the Trottas were nowhere to be found.

The defense met in the hall outside the courtroom a few minutes before the two o'clock reopening of trial. Without the Trottas, Lynn was visibly worried. The question again arose as to whether they ought to have been subpoenaed, but Lynn repeated his objections. If a witness cannot come of his own volition, the chances are great that he will turn against you; the same factors that have kept him away would bring about his intimidation on the stand.

"Then Mr. Lynn took me aside. He told me that I had done fine on the stand, but that he didn't like the way it had gone. Without the Trottas, he didn't think we had much of a chance. He said that. He said it would be risky with that jury. He said maybe the jury would bring in a guilty verdict, and with my former record, the judge would have to send me away, maybe for six months. Even though the judge was sympathetic. He would be forced to, just because of my record. Then he told me that I could plead guilty to a disorderly conduct charge. Wow, I thought. They had brought it all the way down from felonious assault to disorderly conduct. He was very gentle, was Mr. Lynn, that I shouldn't feel bad about pleading guilty, no one would blame me for it, no one. I had done nothing wrong and everyone knew that, he said. And so I had the right to cop a plea. I had the right just to protect myself, so I wouldn't have to go to prison for this. But he said it was strictly up to me. He would go on defending me whatever I decided.

"Well, there wasn't time to think. I just said, No. I wanted to go the whole way. I hadn't done nothing wrong, ever, not in the way a thief or a criminal does. I had a record but I hadn't done nothing wrong. Dumb, maybe. But whatever, I shouldn't go to prison for it. I was going to have to go to prison for what it said on my record—I thought that made it all even worse. What kind of system was it when they start putting the bad mark on you like that policy conviction, like that dumb black cop busting into my apartment saying, 'I'm looking for Bob E. Apt, but if you ain't Bob E. Apt I'm arresting you anyhow because I gotta bring in somebody and you're as good as him!' or getting busted for shooting crap, or even that statutory rape business with Carrie Jones and the baby. You have love relationships with a girl and they tag you with an attempted assault. Here they say you felonious-assaulted a cop but they want to let you off with a disorderly conduct. What I mean is, it didn't make sense any more. Like Mr. Lynn said, I'd done nothing wrong. I wanted to stand up and say that to everyone. I wanted to be a man and act like a man. I had to believe that you could do this in a court of law like you do it in the streets or in your home. Maybe especially in a court of law. I guess what I wanted to think is that when you'd done nothing wrong, you've got to have faith that nothing bad can happen to you."

In the afternoon session, Conrad Lynn was able to secure, through the DA, a copy of the hospital record—which Greenberg permitted to be entered into the court record, but "only that portion of diagnosis and treatment, not history or anything else." In it, Lynn established that Blutcher did indeed receive sixty stitches for multiple skull lacerations and a concussion. During this testimony, Vina Blutcher rose from the spectators' bench and presented Lynn with copies of photographs taken of her brother at the hospital, revealing the gruesome sight of his head two days after the incident. Lynn immediately offered them in evidence. Greenberg, however, found a way of making use of them for his own purposes.

GREENBERG: Who took these pictures?

BLUTCHER: It was taken by a civil lawyer. Mr. Frederick Douglass . . .

GREENBERG: You called him down to the hospital?

BLUTCHER: Well, he was notified because he's a family lawyer.

GREENBERG: . . . You conversed with him in the hospital? You discussed the events of December 3, 1967?

BLUTCHER: We discussed a few of the facts of the case. He asked me certain questions.

GREENBERG: And then he took pictures of your head?

BLUTCHER: Yes.

GREENBERG: And thereafter he instituted a lawsuit in your behalf, did he not?

BLUTCHER: Yes.

GREENBERG: Who is the defendant in that lawsuit, or the defendants?

BLUTCHER: What do you mean?

GREENBERG: Who is the case against?

BLUTCHER: The case is against the City.

GREENBERG: For your injuries?

BLUTCHER: Yes.

GREENBERG: How much are you suing for?

BLUTCHER: One million dollars.

GREENBERG: No further questions.

In the rear of the courtroom, the Court Follower was not surprised. "Well, that blew it. Greenberg demolished him. You could almost see the jury flipping, starting with all those criminal citations and the silly little lie. That million-dollar business was just the icing on the cake. That's the way it goes in a court of law. That's what always grabs you in a trial when you know what to look for. The cops hung together like they'd all been cooking in the same pot of stew, so when you dip the ladle in, it all comes out the same no matter where you dip it. When a kid like that is on trial, even a two-bit DA can find something to make him smell like a rat. Hell, Greenberg is smart and it was there for him on a silver platter."

Lynn despaired. Greenberg had played his hand perfectly. The whole thing had worked out just the way he must have planned, biding his time until he could get Blutcher's pending lawsuit into the testimony, but in a way that suggested he had merely stumbled across it. It was almost as though he knew those pictures were going to be brought into the court just at that moment. This was terribly damaging, Lynn knew: members of the jury are, among other things, taxpayers, and they were going to be asked to acquit a man who might, conceivably, take a million dollars of their money. But even apart from that, the exposure of such a law suit suggested a stigma of acquisitive and vengeful purpose behind the whole defense. It you consider the guilt or innocence of a poor black victim of police brutality, that's one thing. If you think of a man who's going to make a fortune from it, that's another.

He could not help pondering the other possibilities had he not put Blutcher on the stand. There was nothing automatic about such a decision. However, he needed *someone* on that stand to present evidence of what had happened in that store. Would the Trottas alone have been sufficient? Without them, he was forced to use the defendant anyway, and had to suffer the consequences.

It was one of those unfortunate things. Later, he would wonder if he could have handled it all differently.

17

It was at 3:10 on that Wednesday afternoon that Conrad Lynn began his summation to the jury. For twenty-five minutes, he reviewed the testimony and challenged their pending interpretation of it. "You remember . . . two of them grabbed him and slammed him to the floor, and the District Attorney said, 'Well, then that was a fight.' Well, I want you to consider whether that was a fight . . . Or was the only thing happening to him that he was having this rain of blows on him on the floor and it is characterized as a fight. I don't characterize that as a fight. . . . It is for you to draw the conclusions on this conflict of facts. . . ." He was alternately cool, concise, businesslike—and then passionate, indignant, righteous. "This boy is trying to work himself up. He's just a poor black boy in the streets of Brooklyn. He testified that he stays in the store for very long hours. Now, for this minor violation [of the Sabbath Law] was it necessary for the police to go to work on him to such an extent that at the hospital they had to take sixty stitches in his head, or is it more believable that the real reason . . . was because he wasn't coming through with the deal any more, and they were going to teach him a lesson?" Then he reached for the absurd: "Now, would a young man who is running a small grocery store, would it be likely—and you must answer this question for yourselves—would it be likely that such a boy, seeing those three policemen whom he well knows are armed, would he run out from behind the counter, pick up a jar, and throw it unless he was out of his mind?"

Larry Blutcher listened, and in his essential shyness, his eyes dropped to his hands as all those words were being said about him, until, sensing that he might be losing out on something, he raised his glance to the jury and tried to guess their response. What he saw appeared beautiful to him; they were following the short, black lawyer, their attention was complete, they watched him moving slowly along the jury box, his hand brushing gently along the wooden barrier as he passed in front of them, his arm sweeping the room as he gestured toward the defense table, his head cocked in thought like one who was doing far more than making a speech but a man who was trying to get at the very heart of the matter. It was, indeed, beautiful to him, and he thought that there would have to be justice for him after all, it could not possibly end up any other way.

"You are agents to make it clear that we are not yet in a police state; that the citizen by himself, even if no one comes to speak for him, that citizen alone deserves all the considerations that are due, because when the jury makes a judgment on a person, they are affirming once again that although we have all these great difficulties and people from disadvantaged neighborhoods with these obstacles to overcome, he may be sure that there will be no prejudice and no predisposition that because he is the underdog, therefore he must be guilty."

If Lynn had spoken with passion, Greenberg tried wiliness. "You must keep supreme in your mind this: the lives of men are complicated . . . You may decide these police officers are not worthy of belief. You may decide that they have some reason to lie, some axe to grind against the defendant. You may decide that Laurence Blutcher has his own axe to grind; that he's very angry at the police; that he lost his temper in that store, and did a stupid thing, he assaulted a police officer, not because he sat down and thought about doing it, but because he lost his temper and he's a man of action. He's a paratrooper, a man with a war record. He's a young man. You may consider his background to determine whether he's the type of man that would lose his temper or not . . ." He was speaking with gentle, rational, almost pedantic tones, never once raising his voice or adding emphasis to any particular thoughts. Artfully, then, he went from the war record to the criminal record: "Now I don't suggest that you would be so narrow-minded as to say, just because a man ran afoul of the law, that means he would get up on the stand and commit perjury. But it is something to consider. It is part of his background . . ." And from the criminal record, he went on to the civil suit record: "And does the fact that just a few days after the incident, the photographer, who happened to be a lawyer also, happened to talk to him about a million-dollar lawsuit against the city? Does he have dollar signs in his eyes when he testifies before you? Does that color his testimony in any way? Would he lie? That's for you to decide . . ." From the money record to the hospital record: "You must tell us by your verdict, are these police officers rogues? Did they fracture his skull? I believe you now realize that the record shows that was not so." Then, on to the graft-corruption record: "Whether police officers from time immemorial have taken graft is not important. Whether he, Laurence Blutcher, in the past gave graft is not important though that's against the law, also. Forget about that. It doesn't dirty him and it doesn't dirty this police officer."

His conclusion was an appeal for a verdict "without passion, without prejudice. You're not fighting dragons, you're not defending a system, you're not defending a police department, you're not championing the black man, you're not carrying the cudgel of the white cause. The only thing that is on trial is a little incident that happened on December 3, 1967."

It was almost four o'clock when he finished, and the judge dismissed the jury until the following morning when he would charge them as to the law applicable to this case. "The law must be explained to you, the law which will apply to the facts as you will find them, so until then, in all fairness, do not come to any conclusions, do not form any opinions . . ."

"It was weird, the way I felt when I came back home with Monica. We stopped in the store—the same store that was mine, right under the apartment at 960—and bought a six-pack. The man who bought the store from me, he could get a beer license, all right. The beer kept him in business, he told me, even though Ponce across the street was all burnt down. He didn't have to work the way I did. I mean, he had a man in there working for him, sharing the hours. The way I saw the grocery business, the small-store type, it would have to be a man and wife. There just isn't enough action to make it worth hiring someone, even with a beer license. I bought the beer and it suddenly hit me that I'd never asked if the cops had been in there since I'd sold it. I'd never asked if there'd been any Sabbath violations and all that. I'd just never bothered to find out. Here it was, I was living right upstairs, just as I had when they beat me up, and I'd passed the store pretty much every day of my life since, and I'd never asked. But then, they never asked me how I was doing with the case. That's the way it is in the neighborhood sometimes. I guess it's because there's so much trouble going on, nobody thinks much about what's happening to the other guy.

"There was plenty of trouble going inside of me. It was going to be a rough night, and I was full of fear. I tried to get with my faith in Allah, and I prayed some, but I kept thinking about what happened at the trial. The DA had used all that tricknology on the jury and his words stuck in my mind like flies on sticky paper. Like how I was a mad killer with a war record . . .

or a black criminal in the streets and not to be trusted with what I said. I wondered what the jury was thinking about all that, and sure, it made me full of fear. And the way Mr. Lynn seemed upset, especially after the business about the million-dollar lawsuit. I didn't want to go to bed because I knew I wouldn't sleep too good. But I knew that if I stayed up talking about it, that wouldn't do me any good neither. I just didn't know what to think any more. Like I said, I was full of fear.

"Still, I decided one thing: I was not going to cop out. I was going to make the jury go the whole way and reach a verdict. I had come this far, after all these months, I had stood trial like the law says I should, and I was going to stick it out. Innocent or guilty, whatever the jury said, whatever the judge would say, I was going to make them decide. That was what I wanted to do, even if, like Mr. Lynn said, if I lost the gamble I'd have to pay my dues and maybe even go to jail. I said that to myself. I said it out loud: 'I'm going through with it, all the way!' "

Judge Joseph Corso had dinner with his wife and retired to his study, looking forward to a long night's work with the energy and enthusiasm of a young man. He went over his notes of the trial, six huge legal pads full of hurriedly written comments, taking more notes as he reviewed them. Then he pushed them aside for the hard-core decision he would have to make. If it was, indeed, solely up to the jury to determine the guilt or innocence of this young man, his charge to the jury would inevitably reflect his own leanings. In this case, it bothered him. He had to admit he had been taken aback by Lynn's startling motion for dismissal on the grounds that the law at the time of the incident so heavily favored the defendant. Then, too, there was little doubt but that the police had no real concern for the essence of the Sabbath Law. And though he was ready to assume that the police might have been shaking the defendant down, it was difficult for him to believe that they would administer so brutal a beating to protect a mere three-dollar payoff.

His decision, however, had to be made on the interpretation of the law—to give the law to the jury, and to charge them to come to a verdict based on the law as he explained it.

It was approaching midnight when he finally began to write his findings. To start with, he decided to throw out that phase of the indictment referring to the assault in the second degree— when, with intent to prevent a police officer from performing his legal duty, the defendant inflicted injury on that police officer— and that was the only count of the three that was a felony, the other two—resisting arrest and assault in the third degree— being listed as misdemeanors . . .

Larry Blutcher's long night of fear left him more shaky in the morning than Monica had ever seen him. "He could hardly talk. He didn't want to talk, his voice sounded so strange, I thought he might be sick or something. Then, when we were going to the courthouse, he began to kid around some like he usually does, joking and all, but when we got out of the subway and there was the court building, he stopped. He was shaking. I was nervous, too, of course. But it was very different with him. He made me feel very different."

They were there early that Thursday morning, earlier than usual. Blutcher was surprised to see that Conrad Lynn had arrived before them, and that he had already been busy. And when the lawyer pulled him aside, Larry knew exactly what he was going to say.

"Have you thought about this again, Larry?"

He nodded. Yes, he had thought about it plenty.

"You can still plead guilty, you know. The court will reduce to disorderly conduct. It still holds."

"I don't want to do that, Mr. Lynn," he said, but his irresolute tone made him angry with himself. It was as if he were saying one thing and meaning the opposite.

Lynn reached out and rested his hand on Larry's arm, a pacifier before delivering the bad news. "I don't think you realize how much they hurt us yesterday. That testimony was very damaging."

That was what hurt him now, this reminder of yesterday. He didn't want to think of yesterday, but suddenly, he felt the whole impact of it, reliving his feelings as he'd walked to the witness stand, remembering his nervousness as Mr. Lynn had questioned him through all those objections, the way he'd become flustered and how the words had come out sounding wrong. He could actually taste it all again, how the DA had spun him around and how that part of the truth had worked so viciously against him and made him squirm in front of the jury, stripping him of his pride and his sense of righteousness. It was all coming home to him now, this colossal reversal of his expectations. He had foreseen only victory. It was the only way he could have faced the trial. But now he saw that it was not going to be; all these months he had been deluding himself.

What frightened him most was the thought that his tenacity, his doggedness to see this thing through, all his defiance had been rooted in his optimism. He could be brave because he believed he was going to win.

"Larry, you've got to understand, this is not your fault. Nobody is going to condemn you for it. Nobody. You don't have to feel you've done anything wrong . . ."

He stood there listening to words he had heard before, barely conscious of the urgency in Lynn's tone. He had rejected them over and over, and now they were coming at him again and he wasn't so sure any more. He even used to enjoy the thought of facing those words, so solid was his stand against them.

"It's a touchy business," Lynn went on. "I don't know how the judge is going to charge the jury. I don't know what the jury will decide. But you must consider that if they find you guilty, it's going to be tough on the judge . . ."

Larry nodded, turning away to control an impatient, impolite response, knowing what Lynn was going to say in conclusion: "He'll have to send you to jail."

"What I did was, I let the words sink in. I was tired and I didn't know what to think. I don't know, all of a sudden, I just gave into them. I was so mixed up I couldn't think straight. I didn't know what to do. I gave in to the words but I didn't know if I really wanted to. I trusted Mr. Lynn, but it was still up to me. He made that point. It was up to me. I gave in, I said, okay, I would do as he said, plead guilty to the disorderly conduct, and when I said it, finally, I felt relieved. I mean, it was okay. I thought maybe that was what I should have done from the start. At least, that was what I tried to say to myself.

"But then, when Mr. Lynn went up to tell the judge, I knew that no matter how smart I was in doing this, I would always think that I should have stuck it out. I would always think, let them judge me according to their law. Let the judge say what he was going to say to the jury and let the jury decide. That's what I wanted. Then, if they had to, let them send me to jail. Jail ain't so terrible. Even six months of it. Malcolm was in jail for years. Elijah Muhammud was in jail. Lots of good people go to jail. I could go to jail knowing I had done no wrong, but that it was the law that had done the wrong. It wouldn't be so terrible in jail.

"But I'd said okay, and I sat there waiting for what would happen to me next."

Lynn was relieved. He did not want to see the young man go to jail. He had advised the practical solution, all the while admiring Blutcher's determination to take every risk in order to see justice done. Lynn knew what the law was like and what limitations it had in effecting its concept of justice, even its capacity to compensate for these limitations by providing a convenient escape route such as this.

There were times when, if the law didn't acquit you one way, it would let you off in another.

A few minutes later, the judge recessed the jury ("on a matter of consideration of law") and Larry stood before the open court

with his new stance, a guilty man now, and the judge was required to make him sweat through a confession and admission of
his guilt. Larry had to say it, clearly, resolutely, humbly, as if it
were really his truth—that he had violated the law and was
therefore subject to such penalty as the law might prescribe, that
he had used profane and obscene language to the policemen on
that day in December 1967, that he had fought with them, resisted them, yes, even injured one.

Guilty, yes. Blutcher confessed to it a dozen times in those torturous five minutes, in answer to every question by the judge, repeated for clarity in a dozen different forms, abetted then by the
Assistant DA himself: "I respectfully ask Your Honor to ask the
defendant if he is pleading guilty because he is guilty or merely
to escape the possible greater punishment of being found guilty
under the indictment." And the Judge rammed it home once
more: "Are you pleading guilty because you are in fact guilty?"

"Yes, I am."

"You're not doing it because of any fear of anything else?"

"No, I'm not."

"You're doing it because you are in fact guilty."

"Yes. Yes."

He told himself, it was all okay. Like Mr. Lynn had told him.
Like others had told him. It was the way of the world, you figure
the angles and you make your deals, and if you play your cards
right, even a poor black man gets a break every now and then.
That's the way they were all figuring it, wasn't it? The words
were swirling around him, the judge, the old clerk of court, Mr.
Lynn, they were putting it all together and wrapping it up, they
were waiving the forty-eight-hour delay for notice of sentencing
so that the whole business could be over right then and there.
He barely listened. It was like they were saying the same words
over and over, and then the judge looked down on him and he
was standing there stiffly before him, and the final words were
spoken: ". . . It is the sentence of this court that on the violation

classified as disorderly conduct to which the defendant pleaded guilty that the sentence of this court shall be unconditional release." He heard Mr. Lynn say "Thank you, Judge," and his body began to tremble, the sweat to gather in the back of his neck, and he felt sick. It was all over. Unconditional release. No parole. No fine. No suspended sentence. It was just like being innocent. It was his reward for playing the game the way he was supposed to.

But it didn't make sense, it didn't make any sense at all. Not really. He had fought, one way or another, all these long months to prove his innocence according to the system, and now the system lets him off free when he falsely admits his guilt. It was all a crazy set of lies, right from the beginning. Lies and hypocrisies. He had slaved in a grocery store because he thought that was the way to make good, playing by the rules, but there was another set of rules, the policeman's rules, and they had beaten him up because he did not play by them. And when he tried to clear himself by the honest rules, they told him there was still another set of rules, and he had finally knuckled under to them. That's what he had done. It was just like paying off the cops, then, wasn't it? Isn't that what he had done here today? Isn't that what he was being rewarded for? When he'd refused, isn't that what had made the cops so mad at him? Just like now, as Mr. Lynn had told him, cop the plea or else the court will get mad and send you away for six months. So he stood there shaking and sweating, once again full of fear, because he was afraid that it was all too far beyond his understanding, that he would never really understand, and it made him sick.

If the system doesn't beat you one way, it beats you in another.

"Then they had the jury come back in, and the judge told them how they had served so well, and even though they were not being called on to deliver a verdict, they had done their job. Then he closed the case, just like that. He never told them how it was settled. He didn't even give them a hint. He sent them back to the jury pool, maybe to serve on another case, and they would never find out what had happened to me.

"And then I thought, they didn't know what they would have decided if they had to decide, and I would never know, either."